BRUCE WEBER'S
★ INSIDE ★
PRO FOOTBALL
◇ 1991 ◇

SCHOLASTIC INC.
New York Toronto London Auckland Sydney

PHOTO CREDITS

ISBN 0-590-44707-6

CONTENTS

INTRODUCTION
A New World Order

The months of preparation are finally, thankfully, over. The roster moves; the Plan B signings; the draft; the minicamps, maxicamps, quarterback camps, rookie camps, and training camps. Now comes the longest final exam in the world: 16 tests in 17 weeks with a late-January trip to Minneapolis as the reward. Dress warm!

The haves, of course, still have it. But some of the have-nots are on the brink of becoming haves, too. The Dallas Cowboys haven't been have-nots for very long. But the 'Pokes have gone from 1–15 to play-off contenders in rapid-fire order. Now, with sound planning from coach Jimmy Johnson and his staff, the Cowboys could find themselves in serious contention by the time the postseason Roman numerals read XXVIII or XXIX.

The Atlanta Falcons have been have-nots a lot longer, but those days may soon be over. The Falcons, who move into their spiffy new Georgia Dome home next fall, have rebuilt by wheeling and dealing draft picks for the last couple of years. They're not ready yet, but by Super Bowl XXX? Could be.

In the AFC, the Bills are planning on another January shot against the NFC's best, and off the total domination of their conference last year, it's a real possibility.

The Raiders, with their ex-49er stars Roger Craig and Ronnie Lott, should challenge, even without Bo Jackson. But Marty Schottenheimer's Kansas City Chiefs will make it plenty tough for L.A. to get out of the AFC West. San Diego will be better, Denver can't get worse, and Seattle is treading water.

The AFC Central is the model of inconsistency. You never know which Bengals or which Oilers will show up on any Sunday. Pittsburgh is more consistent, but less talented. Cleveland doesn't qualify in any department.

Miami will give Buffalo all they can handle in the East, with the Jets improved, the Colts trying to keep Jeff George alive, and the Patriots on the long road back.

The NFC East should be a four-way battle, maybe even five-way if Phoenix rallies.

In the Central, everyone tries to catch Chicago, with an edge to Detroit and Minnesota. With their quarterback situation calmer than it has been in years, the Bears should be in good shape.

In the West, the Rams are going to be better (so help us, John Robinson), Atlanta will be *much* better, and New Orleans, if it can find a quarterback, will be downright dangerous. Still, no one in the division touches the Niners.

Let the games begin!

— Bruce Weber

Cover Story
LAWRENCE TAYLOR
NEW YORK GIANTS

They say he has lost a step. His former coach, Bill Parcells, concedes that he gets beat up a little more than he used to and that it takes him longer to bounce back.

But teams preparing to play the Super Bowl champion New York Giants know that they must begin their offensive plan by figuring some way to stop Lawrence Taylor. "He doesn't look like he's slowed down to me," says Randall Cunningham, who has dodged L.T. throughout his career.

"I've learned that I have to play within the system now," says L.T., who went without a sack for seven straight weeks last season. "At my age, you just can't go crazy on every play anymore. But I'm not ready to retire, and you can tell by the way the opponents put at least two guys on me that they don't think I'm ready to retire either."

The Giants defense, which was the key factor in the team's march to the Super Bowl XXV title last season, is now less predictable than it was in L.T.'s youth. They blitz less but enjoy it more, with a controlled pass-rush and tighter coverages. But everyone knows that Taylor still has what it takes. His rivals named him to the Pro Bowl for a tenth straight year in '90. His next stop, of course, is the Hall of Fame.

National Football League All-Pro Team

Wide Receiver
JERRY RICE
San Francisco 49ers

Ask for a refund. You shouldn't have to pay for this page. Anyone who has ever watched even a few games of NFL football can name the best wide receiver. When you pick your All-Pro team, you simply start with Mr. Automatic, Jerry Rice.

It will be interesting to see what happens as the Forty Niners begin to revamp their team. With Roger Craig and Ronnie Lott gone, other changes seem inevitable. But when San Fran plans its offense of the nineties, it must begin with Rice, the most dangerous player in the game.

Despite double and triple coverage, Rice still manages to find a way to get open. His 1990 numbers were typical; a league-leading 100 catches (18 more than runner-up Andre Rison) for a league-leading 1,502 yards (208 more than runner-up Henry Ellard) and a league-leading 13 TDs. His five-TD outburst at Atlanta last year showed everyone why he's No 1.

"It's a gift," says Rice. "I see the field well and I always know where the pressure is coming from, even when it's from behind."

No matter what changes Niners coach George Seifert makes in his team's offense, he won't forget that Jerry Rice has produced 83 TDs in 92 games.

Wide Receiver
ANDRE RISON
ATLANTA FALCONS

When the Indianapolis Colts decided they needed Jeff George to be their quarterback, they dealt Chris Hinton and Andre Rison to the Atlanta Falcons for the first draft pick. Hinton was a veteran Pro Bowl tackle; Rison was a decent wide receiver. That was last year; this is this year. This year Andre Rison is one of the most feared wide receivers in pro football.

"I'd like to be Jerry Rice someday," says the flashy, cocky, 5'11", 185-pound Rison. "Hey, he's a Hall-of-Famer, no question. But I think I can be as good — maybe even better."

Self-confidence is something that Rison stores in buckets. The Falcons didn't name him "Showtime" for nothing. "I can dish it out as well as I can take it," says Andre. He can also catch the football — 82 times for 1,208 yards and 10 TDs in 1990. Only Rice had more receptions (100) than the one-time Michigan State star. And you've gotta believe that if Andre had Joe Montana, not Chris Miller, throwing to him, the difference might be even smaller.

The man who made his highlight-zone post-TD dance a crowd favorite in Atlanta (it's out in '91, according to the new NFL rules) is a surefire Rison star.

Tight End
RODNEY HOLMAN
CINCINNATI BENGALS

"I know when Rodney Holman became a frightening tight end," says Cincinnati Bengals quarterback Boomer Esiason. "We were playing Kansas City a couple of years ago and whenever I looked downfield for Rodney, a Chiefs linebacker was draped all over his back. The highest compliment you can pay a tight end is holding him."

It was a long time coming. When Rodney arrived in Cincinnati from Tulane in 1982, he caught only five passes during his first two seasons. Ever since, the fearsome blocker and feared receiver has played an increasingly major role in the high-powered Bengal offense. In 1988 he made the Pro Bowl for the first time; and in '89, grabbing 50 passes for 739 yards and 9 TDs, he earned a repeat Pro Bowl appearance. Rodney made it three Pro Bowls in a row last year when he caught 40 passes for 596 yards (a 14.9 yards per catch average) and 5 TDs. He's a major-league threat.

One of seven sons and two daughters of an Ypsilanti, MI, cement mason, Holman goes about his business quietly and seriously. "He's not one of those guys who gets hung up on the hype," says teammate David Fulcher. Bengal head coach Sam Wyche loves Holman's dedication to his work.

Offensive Tackle
JIM LACHEY
WASHINGTON REDSKINS

If there were ever any doubts about Jim Lachey's ability, the Redskins tackle laid them all to rest in 1990. He enters the new season as our All-Pro and, arguably, the best tackle in the NFL.

Who says so? The rest of the NFL. When the league's players voted for their Pro Bowl choices late last season, no tackle garnered as many votes as the 6'6", 290-pounder from Ohio State. He was also the NFC's Lineman of the Year. When he was named as the NFC's Offensive Player of the Week after the week-12 games, he became only the second offensive lineman to win that honor in six years!

"I can't believe anyone could have a better year than Jim had last year," says Redskins offensive line coach Jim Hanifan, who should know. "He's determined to be the best player he can possibly be — and I believe he's going to get even better."

The 'Skins parted with quarterback Jay Schroeder to get Lachey right after the 1988 season opener. Jim had played in a couple of Pro Bowls for San Diego before being dealt to the Raiders earlier that year. After one solid but unspectacular season in Washington, Jim regained his All-Pro form in '89 and hasn't been headed since.

Offensive Tackle
ANTHONY MUNOZ
CINCINNATI BENGALS

It's getting tougher these days. The knees ache, the shoulders are sore. To maintain his quickness, he has had to drop a few pounds, which reduces his power. But as he has for the better part of the last decade, Cincinnati Bengal Anthony Munoz remains the standard by which all NFL offensive tackles are measured. And though Munoz may have only a season or two left in him, he should remain the standard well into the next century.

At a position where players are often chosen mainly because of their size, the 6'6", 284-pound Munoz is a complete athlete. His quick feet and smooth movements have made him the game's premier tackle.

A first-round draft pick (the No. 3 selection overall) from Southern Cal in the 1980 draft, Munoz has been on 10 straight Pro Bowl rosters. "Anthony busts his chops on every play of every game," raves his No. 1 fan, Bengals coach Sam Wyche. "Whatever we ask him to do, he does, and he's a leader both on and off the field. They don't come any better."

The veteran Munoz has one more career goal: a Super Bowl victory. "We've been there once and lost," he says. "I want to go back there and win."

6

Guard
BRUCE
MATTHEWS
HOUSTON OILERS

The best right guard in football may turn out to be the best center in football. The Oilers' Bruce Matthews, who joins with left guard Mike Munchak to form perhaps the best guard combo in the NFL, was thrust into emergency service at center late last season (again!). And unless a new pivot man pops up in Houston's summer drills, Oiler boss Jack Pardee may locate Matthews there again in '91.

"Bruce wasn't happy playing there," says Houston offensive line coach Bob Young, "but he did it for the team. He's a surefire All-Pro no matter where we play him."

The 6'5", 291-pound Matthews, brother of longtime All-Pro linebacker Clay Matthews, anchors an outstanding offensive line that does a superlative job protecting run-and-shoot QB Warren Moon. That he has become a role model for linemen all over the NFL is no accident. "No one outworks him," says guardmate Munchak. "Despite all the honors that come his way, he only wants to get better."

Switching positions isn't anything new for Matthews, who played left tackle back in 1986. "I don't know if it's a plus or not," he says, "but if it happens, I've got to readjust and do the job."

RANDALL McDANIEL

MINNESOTA VIKINGS

When the opponents you face in practice every day are named Chris Doleman and Keith Millard, how much harder can it possibly get on game day? For the Minnesota Vikings' Randall McDaniel, Sunday is the easy day.

When the 6'4", 275-pound McDaniel arrived in the Viking camp from Arizona State (as Minnesota's first-round pick in the 1988 draft), coach Jerry Burns figured he was at least three years away from becoming a solid pro. "It usually takes that long for an offensive lineman to develop," says the head Viking. "But this guy put it together quicker than anyone I've seen."

By the end of his sophomore season, he was in the Pro Bowl (only four other Vikings in history had made it that quickly); and now, with three years under his belt, he's at the head of the class of NFL guards.

"I still have some things to learn," says McDaniel. "This game is always changing, and you must keep up. The main thing is working with the rest of the line to make sure you function as a unit."

What else is in the McDaniel scouting report? Just one more thing: If you invite Randall to a party, make sure you have plenty of pizza. He loves the stuff!

Center
KENT HULL
BUFFALO BILLS

It took a while, but Kent Hull is there. Finally. The best center in football.

A high school quarterback, tight end, and middle linebacker in Greenwood, MS, Hull became a center in his senior year and has been polishing his game ever since.

Hull has paid his dues. "I've never been on a team that has won it all," he says, though his Bills came within a couple of feet of pulling out Super Bowl XXV. "That's what I'd really like," he says. Another shot could come as early as next January.

Meanwhile, he'll have to content himself with wearing the crown as the NFL's best pivot man. "I think he's number one," raves his quarterback, Jim Kelly. "I know a lot of NFL nose guards will agree. Kent is so strong that he can take a defender anywhere he wants to take him. And he's a wonderful leader."

The 6'5", 275-pounder has everything a coach looks for in a center: strength, agility, quickness, and smarts. Bills offensive line coach Tom Bresnahan swears Hull functions like an extra coach on the field.

"I strive for perfection," says Kent. "I know I have room for improvement, particularly on running plays. I've always wanted to be the best at everything I've done."

Quarterback
RANDALL CUNNINGHAM
PHILADELPHIA EAGLES

This is his year! It should have come sooner. Randall Cunningham, perhaps the finest athlete in the NFL, is ready to become its top quarterback.

Every coach who has been forced to contend with Cunningham has a story about some unbelievable feat pulled off by rangy Randall. Sympathetic fans can feel sorry for NFL East field bosses, who need to prepare for the wondrous one twice a year.

"He puts pressure on your defense every play," says ex-Giants coach Bill Parcells. "You never know what he's going to do and that makes him especially tough." Washington's field boss, Joe Gibbs, agrees, saying, "If you let him get out of the pocket, he can kill you."

A typical example: Last December 2, Buffalo's Bruce Smith had Randall dead to rights in the end zone, blowing in from the blind side. Somehow Cunningham ducked the rush, rolled left, and threw 58 yards into a stiff wind to WR Fred Barnett. Barnett split the defenders and wound up with an amazing 95-yard TD pass.

Whether he runs the ball (3,437 yards on 486 carries in six seasons) or throws it (3,466 yards and 30 TDs last season), Randall is football's most dangerous man.

Running Back
THURMAN THOMAS
BUFFALO BILLS

Giants fans have this recurring nightmare: It's Super Bowl XXV, and the Bills' Scott Norwood is lining up to try the game-winning field goal. Then, mysteriously, the officials find that a minute had mistakenly disappeared from the game clock. So now there's 1:04 to go. Jim Kelly pitches the ball to Thurman Thomas and. . . . You can imagine the rest.

Other backs have gotten more exposure the last couple of seasons, but none has been more productive than the Bills' super back. Check these numbers: 1,297 yards rushing in '90, tops in the AFC; 1,829 yards rushing and receiving, tops in the NFL; 3,742 yards rushing and receiving in two seasons.

Thomas held out of training camp last summer, eventually negotiating a $1-million-a-year contract. It didn't take him long to prove he was worth it. He ran for 84 yards and grabbed 9 passes in the team's opener, then rushed for 214 yards in an early-season game.

Finally, there was the Super Bowl (15 rushes for 135 yards and a 31-yard TD scamper, 5 catches for 55 yards) that, despite the 20–19 deficit, made Thomas a household word in households everywhere.

Running Back
BARRY
SANDERS
DETROIT LIONS

It should be an interesting year in Detroit. With run-and-shoot pioneer Mouse Davis off to the WLAF, will the Lions make any significant changes in their offense?

Any way head coach Wayne Fontes decides to go, however, he'd better make special plans for Barry Sanders, probably the most gifted running back in the NFL.

Sanders bounced onto the scene a couple of seasons back, gained 1,470 yards his first year (10 yards behind league-leader Christian Okoye) and 1,304 yards last year (to lead the league). The Lions' spread offense, which spreads the defense, has played a major role. Sanders gets the ball on draws, traps, and counters that enable him to get the most of out of his considerable talent. For his career, he averages better than five yards a carry; that's a Hall-of-Fame number.

Until the Hall calls, however, Sanders has plenty to do. Add brains to his great running ability. He reads the defense, then uses his fabulous stop-start moves to pull away from tacklers who had him.

Trivia buffs will be pleased to know that the man Sanders beat for the 1990 league rushing title (by only seven yards) was his college teammate Thurman Thomas.

Defensive End
BRUCE SMITH
BUFFALO BILLS

If you ever have a question about Bruce Smith's ability, all you have to do is ask Bruce. There's no doubt about what the Buffalo Bills' premier defensive end is: big, tough, quick, and smart. The one thing he is *not* is modest.

Back in December, when the Bills were preparing to meet the New York Giants in what turned out to be a Super Bowl preview, Smith announced for all to know that he — and not the Giants' Lawrence Taylor — was the game's top defensive player. L.T. argued then, but after New York's Supe XXV victory, had to admit that Smith was pretty darn good.

A four-time Pro Bowler, Smith had his best season in '90 with a career-high 19 sacks (second only to Kansas City's Derrick Thomas) and a safety in the Super Bowl. More important, he substantially upgraded his defense against the run and is now a complete player. His game has finally caught up to his mouth.

"I think I'm the best in the league," the 6'4", 275-pounder says, flat out. "I've worked hard to get to this point and even I'm a little surprised that I've done as well as I have." That Smith has the courage to "tell it like it is" comes as absolutely no surprise!

Defensive End
REGGIE WHITE
PHILADELPHIA EAGLES

When the Philadelphia Eagles are in trouble, they know what to do. They turn Reggie White loose.

The man they call the Minister of Defense remains virtually unstoppable at a time when other sack-masters are being frustrated by blocking schemes specially geared to stop them. "In the past," says White, "I've been double-teamed frequently and triple-teamed occasionally. These days, I'm triple-teamed much of the time. If I come on the inside, I have to beat the tackle, take on the guard, and then there's usually a back waiting for me. It's tough."

But that doesn't stop the deeply religious 6'5", 285-pounder with eye-popping speed (4.9 seconds for 40 yards). He has a bag of tricks that would make a magician jealous. But when he salts the bag away and just charges straight ahead, he may be even more dangerous.

Although you probably won't hear it from White, NFL referees studying the fine art of holding by offensive linemen should review Philadelphia game films. "I can't believe what they do to Reggie," says new Eagles coach Rich Kotite. "He deserves all the credit he gets."

Defensive Tackle
RAY CHILDRESS
HOUSTON OILERS

Jack Pardee knew he was taking a chance. For five seasons after he left Texas A&M, Ray Childress was the best darn defensive end they'd seen in Houston in a long time. Even in 1989, when he missed the last three games (the Oilers lost them all) with a broken leg, he was the team's leading sacker (8½) and tackling lineman (57). But Pardee restored a four-man front to the Oilers in '90 and picked up Ezra Johnson, whose specialty was playing the outside. Bang! Ray Childress was playing inside. By midseason, Houston sportswriters were looking for all-timers to compare to Childress. The name most often heard was Bob Lilly, the Dallas Cowboy Hall-of-Famer. The company, for Childress, was impressive.

For the 6'6", 272-pounder, the switch to the inside was a breeze. For the sixth straight year, he led Oiler linemen in tackles (85) and also rang up eight sacks.

"Do I admire that guy?" asks Oiler defensive end William Fuller, who plays just outside Childress's right shoulder. "He never shuts down his motor. He's incredible." Coach Jack Pardee agrees: "Ray never lets down. When some guys get tired, they rest. Not Ray. He plays through it, turning it up a notch if necessary."

Outside Linebacker
DERRICK THOMAS
KANSAS CITY CHIEFS

The Kansas City Chiefs waited until their 30th season (1989) to pick a linebacker in the first round of the NFL draft. But when the Arrowhead gang finally took the plunge, they knew what they were doing. All Derrick Thomas has done since the Chiefs plucked him off the Alabama campus is dominate football games, including one mighty, hard-to-believe seven-sack game in a 17–16 loss to Seattle last season.

It was just one more frightening performance by the 6'3", 234-pounder who replaced Cornelius Bennett in the Alabama defense. Speed is the key to his game. He's so quick that he can usually take an outside line and still get to the quarterback.

But the two-time Pro Bowler has worked on his inside moves, too. Offenses that thought they could stop Thomas by forcing him to the inside are just plain out of luck. His league-leading 21 sacks last year were more than double his 1989 team-leading mark of 10.

Though Derrick is occasionally troubled by runs right at him, he's so good at pursuit, shedding blocks, and getting to the ball that he is virtually impossible to stop.

Is Thomas the next L.T.? Could be.

Outside Linebacker
CHARLES HALEY
SAN FRANCISCO 49ERS

As NFL opponents have discovered, it's awfully tough to get a handle on Charles Haley. Though there was no three-peat for his San Francisco 49ers last season, outside 'backer Haley continued to haunt rival quarterbacks and cause sleepless nights for coaches all over the league.

A dominant player in a Division I-AA college program (James Madison University in Virginia), Haley lasted until the fourth round of the NFL draft in 1986. Some folks openly questioned how effective he'd be against much tougher competition.

The doubters obviously didn't know Charles Haley. Intense and hardworking, Haley has become the brawn of the Niners' defense, leading the club in sacks in each of his five NFL seasons, including 16 last year. And he's just as good against the run.

At 6'5" and 230 pounds, Haley spends almost as much time as a down lineman as he does as a stand-up linebacker. That created communications problems for Charles, who felt obligated to attend both linebacker and defensive line meetings. The Niners' solution was to bring in a special coach just for Haley. Now the only confusion belongs to opponents who can't figure out a way to block the big guy.

Inside Linebacker
PEPPER JOHNSON
NEW YORK GIANTS

Say "Giants linebacker" and you instantly think Lawrence Taylor. Maybe Carl Banks. Joining that crew seemed to be the quickest way to become the Unknown Soldier.

But Pepper Johnson is not unknown anymore. A part-timer as recently as 1989, the ex-Ohio State star (and Giants second-round draft pick in '85) finally won a full-time role and quickly showed that he was every bit the equal of the big-name guys.

"Pepper is playing as well as any inside 'backer in the league," said Randall Cunningham, the Eagles quarterback, who has the best possible view. "It's Johnson and L.T. who hold the Giants together."

The fact is, Johnson may well be better against the run than the much-honored Taylor. And his pass coverage, a weakness in the past, has vastly improved. "Pepper is uncanny," says L.T. "He always seems to show up where the offense doesn't want to see him. And then he simply makes the play."

There was never any doubt about Johnson's talent. Pepper, who got his nickname by pouring pepper on his Corn Flakes as a kid, needed to grow up. "He's just more determined and dedicated now," says former Giants coach Bill Parcells.

Inside Linebacker
MIKE SINGLETARY
CHICAGO BEARS

Mike Singletary says this is his last season. It's hard to believe. The 32-year-old Chicago middle man is still at the top of his game — he played in his eighth Pro Bowl last February — and with an improved cast around him, he could probably go on for a few more years at least. So why would he pack it in after the '91 campaign? Probably because like the cartoon world's Yogi, Mike is just a little bit smarter than your average Bear.

There must be something to that. At only 230 pounds and only six feet tall, the one-time Baylor-Bear-turned-Chicago-Bear is just a bit undersized for an NFL inside 'backer. He has reached his exalted position through a combination of smarts, guts, and strength.

Deeply religious and a major contributor to his Chicago community, Singletary may well be looking to a coaching career as his playing days dwindle. He will be working with Bear coaches in his spare time (ha!) this season as he begins to look ahead.

"The Lord gave me just enough ability so that I don't let down," says Singletary. "And then He blessed me with the wisdom to understand what I have. I'm deeply grateful for both."

19

Cornerback
ALBERT LEWIS
KANSAS CITY CHIEFS

Numbers freaks, those folks who spend Monday mornings scanning the weekly statistics reports, would never find a spot on their fantasy squads for Kansas City cornerback Albert Lewis. His two interceptions in '90 ranked him fifth on his own team. In fact, the lanky Lewis has only eight INTs in the last four years. But pro football insiders insist that the former Grambling star is the best man-for-man coverage back in the league.

The word has gone out to NFL quarterbacks facing the Chiefs: If you see No. 29 in the neighborhood, hold onto the football. As a result, Lewis is rarely tested. The 6'2" Lewis, one of the tallest corners in the game, is blessed with great speed, particularly on longer runs. When the ball is in the air, he closes to the receiver extremely well, and on those rare occasions when he's beaten, he recovers beautifully. He's excellent in providing run support, and there aren't many better open-field tacklers.

If you plan to be in Honolulu next February, you should have an excellent shot at getting Lewis's autograph. Albert has made four straight trips to the NFL Pro Bowl, and barring injury, another visit in '92 seems like a sure thing.

Cornerback
ROD WOODSON
PITTSBURGH STEELERS

Forgive Rod Woodson if he casts an envious eye toward Barcelona next summer. No, the WLAF's Dragons hold no attraction for Woodson. But when the '92 Olympics open in Spain, Rod will be watching the top hurdlers, knowing that he could have been one of them had he not chosen to play pro football.

He made the right choice. His million-dollar salary aside (and that's not easy to do), Rod has become a premier NFL cornerback, the leader of Pittsburgh's top-rated defense, and one of the NFL's top punt and kickoff returners.

"Rod Woodson is a super player, the best corner in football right now," says Mel Blount, a Steelers all-timer and a Hall-of-Fame cornerback himself. "Rod is miles ahead of me, and he's going to get better."

When Pittsburgh players elected Woodson the team's MVP last winter, Woodson was properly humble. "Being selected by your peers is the highest possible honor," Rod said. But it was richly deserved. Woodson topped the Steelers with five interceptions, was fifth in tackles with 66, and ranked second in the AFC in kickoff-returns and third in punt-returns. Not bad for an old hurdler!

Strong Safety
JOEY BROWNER
MINNESOTA VIKINGS

When times are the toughest, the great ones come through. For the Vikings' Joey Browner, things were never tougher than they were last October. His team, the defending Central champion, was going down the drain, losing six of its first seven games. Then, to make matters worse, Joey's mom died after a long illness.

The eight-year veteran was devastated. Joey was extremely close to his mother and he mourned her loss deeply. But when he returned to the ball club (he missed a week of practices during the mourning period), he turned his All-Pro game up a notch.

That's when the darkness of October turned to the gleam of November. In four games, Joey made 27 tackles (23 of them solos), picked off four interceptions (including a 26-yarder for a TD), and for good measure, threw in a QB sack on a safety blitz. It was no accident that the Vikes won four straight and went from a dismal 1–6 to a contending 5–6.

Though he's quiet and soft-spoken, Browner is a key leader for Minnesota. "Some guys lead by talking," says long-time teammate Carl Lee. "But Joey leads by doing what he does on the field — and the rest of us follow."

Free Safety
MARK CARRIER
CHICAGO BEARS

If Penn State is Linebacker U., then Southern Cal is the Safety Institute. And if his rookie year was any indication, the Bears' Mark Carrier, the latest product of the USC back-liner finishing school, may well become the best of the best.

Carrier, the sixth choice in the 1990 draft, follows in the footsteps of such Trojan All-Pros as Ronnie Lott, Joey Browner, Dennis Smith, Timmy McDonald, and others.

Not only did Carrier make an instant impact in the NFL a year ago, he even became the target of the rules committee during the off-season. The Bears actually negotiated Carrier's contract before drafting him, assuring that he'd be in camp when drills opened. It turned out to be a good deal for both sides, but the lawmakers put an end to this procedure, beginning in '91.

Carrier learned the Bears' system quickly, and by opening day, his rookie jitters were long gone. He wound up with 10 interceptions, two more than the next thief.

"I can't tell you how happy I am with Mark," said Bear boss Mike Ditka. "He's always ready to sacrifice his body and do anything to make a tackle. He sure learned the Bear tradition in a hurry."

Houston's run-and-shoot QB Warren Moon has the Oilers in orbit, ready for another run at the AFC Central crown.

American Football Conference Team Previews

AFC East
BUFFALO BILLS
1990 Finish: First
1991 Prediction: First

Shane Conlan   **Jim Kelly**

A Super Bowl visit does not a dynasty make. But Marv Levy's Bills, playing in one of the NFL's weaker divisions, appear to be in good shape as they try for a second straight trip. The Buffalo roster is deep, reasonably young, and mostly free of people with problems.

QB Jim Kelly is clearly at the top of his game, off a superb year: 219 of 346 for 2,829 yards, 24 TDs, and only nine interceptions. His final QB rating (101.2) made him one of only five QBs with a rating that was higher than 100 (Snake Stabler, Bert Jones, Dan Marino, and Joe Montana were the others) since the NFL started ranking passers in 1973. Backup Frank Reich continues to impress whenever he plays.

All-Pro RB Thurman Thomas (271 carries

for 1,297 yards, 49 catches for 532 yards, 13 TDs) scared the living daylights out of the Giants in the Super Bowl, just as he did every other opponent the Bills played. And there's loads of depth with Kenneth Davis and Don Smith. Look for Carwell Gardner to push Jamie Mueller at fullback.

Speedy Andre Reed (71 catches for 945 yards, 8 TDs) is one of the NFL's premier wide receivers, but at age 35, James Lofton could have problems. Don Beebe's health is a question. Keith McKeller (34 for 464) has become a top TE.

The offensive line should return intact, with Ts Will Wolford and Howard Ballard, Gs Jim Ritcher and John Davis, and All-Pro C Kent Hull. Depth may be a concern here.

When the Giants held the ball for more than 40 minutes during the Super Bowl, the Bills run defense became suspect. But All-Pro DRE Bruce Smith is outstanding, and DLE Leon Seals and NT Jeff Wright really pressure enemy QBs.

The LBs are the strength of the defense, led by outside 'backers Cornelius Bennett and Darryl Talley and inside men Shane Conlan and Ray Bentley. The best quartet in the game? Probably.

If any area concerns Levy, it's his secondary, which explains the selection of Henry Jones in the draft. SS Leonard Smith has lost a step or so, and FS Mark Kelso has been hurt. CBs Kirby Jackson and Nate Odomes are adequate and maybe just a hair more.

AFC East
MIAMI DOLPHINS
1990 Finish: Second
1991 Prediction: Second

Dan Marino

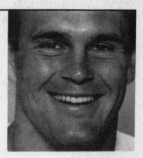

John Offerdahl

For years, despite the most fearsome passing game in the league, the Dolphins floundered. (Sorry about that!) Now, having rediscovered defense and a running game, the Fish are back.

Not that there isn't room for improvement. QB Dan Marino (306 for 531, 3,563 yards, 21 TDs) is still about as dangerous as ever, which means Miami games aren't over 'til they're over. Scott Secules who, like Marino, has a strong arm and quick release, backs up, with Scott Mitchell in the wings.

Marino to Mark Clayton — that's the NFL's all-time top scoring combination. They've connected for scores 65 times. But Clayton is 30 now, and the other "Marks Brother," Mark Duper, is 32. That means that top rookie Randal Hill may need to step in soon. Pro Bowl TE Ferrell Edmunds (31 for 446) is a talent who should get even better. Ex-Patriot Plan B TE Eric Sievers is a fine addition.

RB Sammie Smith (226 carries for 831 yards), like the little girl in the nursery rhyme, is very good when he's good and just so-so when he's not. FB Tony Paige (32 for 95) doesn't get the credit he deserves. The rest of the crowd is closely matched.

Miami retooled the left side of its line in '90 with rookies LT Richmond Webb (a Pro Bowler) and LG Keith Sims. Now attention may be focused on the right side, where RG Harry Galbreath is probably too small, and RT Mark Dennis isn't a great run-blocker. Watch for Jeff Dellenbach to challenge for a starting role. Jeff Uhlenhake returns at center.

Pro Bowl DRE Jeff Cross, who started strong and finished slow, keys a defensive line that includes DLE T.J. Turner and NT Shawn Lee. Ex-Bear Plan B pickup Terry Price could fit here.

LILB John Offerdahl leads an improved linebacker crew that includes Hugh Green, David Griggs, and E.J. Junior on the outside and Cliff Odom on the inside. An improved rush from this group is essential.

With LCB Tim McKyer gone to Atlanta, ex-Bear Vestee Jackson could move right in. RCB J.B. Brown is much improved. SS Jarvis Williams and highly ranked FS Louis Oliver are first-rate.

AFC East
NEW YORK JETS
1990 Finish: Fourth
1991 Prediction: Third

Al Toon   **Bill Pickel**

The Jets, who spent 1990 on a roller coaster, ended on an upturn that may continue in '91. Though coach Bruce Coslet had some difficulty dealing with the New York press, he had no trouble leading his team. That's a step forward for the Jets.

Courageous QB Ken O'Brien (226 for 411, 2,855 yards, 13 TDs) survived a challenge from Tony Eason (who's now gone) and remains the No. 1 man. Backup Troy Taylor or top pick Browning Nagle may be the QB of the future. But an offensive-line upgrade is the key for any of them.

What saves the passing game is a solid set of receivers, led by superstar Al Toon (57 for 757, 6 TDs) and '90 rookie Rob Moore (41 for 692, 6 TDs). There's depth, too, with Chris Burkett, Terance Mathis, and JoJo

Townsell. Things aren't nearly as good at TE, where Mark Boyer (40 for 334) returns, along with Chris Dressel.

As many holes as the Jets have, they're loaded with running backs. Blair Thomas (123 for 620 yards) delivered as promised and should continue to improve. Hefty running mate Brad Baxter (124 for 539) should pair with Thomas for a long time. Comeback kid Freeman McNeil and Johnny Hector still have some yards left.

New York is set in the middle of the offensive line, with C Jim Sweeney and Gs Mike Haight, Dave Cadigan, and Dwayne White. The tackles, however, don't match up, with Jeff Criswell and Brett Miller the returning regulars. Ex-Chief Irv Eatman and ex-Seahawk Ron Mattes could help.

The Jets' too-small defensive line should be aided by ex-Raider Bill Pickel and ex-Dolphin John Bosa. New York needs a pass-rush, something it didn't get from DEs Jeff Lageman and Marvin Washington and DTs Scott Mersereau and Dennis Byrd.

The linebackers may be even weaker. Troy Johnson and Joe Mott return outside, with Kyle Clifton in the middle.

Coslet was delighted with his CBs, rookie Tony Stargell and James Hasty, in '90. But FS Erik McMillan has had better years, and SS Brian Washington didn't impress. McMillan simply must rebound.

The Jets' MVP? Maybe it's the NFL's oldest player, 39-year-old PK Pat Leahy who hit 23 of 26 field-goal attempts.

AFC East
INDIANAPOLIS COLTS
1990 Finish: Third
1991 Prediction: Fourth

Eugene Daniel

Jeff George

Quarterback Jeff George might soon show up on a new quiz show, "Where's My Line?" The Colts front five is absolutely dreadful, and on any given Sunday, George might think he's stuck in a war zone.

The Colts have other problems, too. The defensive line is shaky; the secondary, weak; the offensive line, a disaster area.

When we last saw Indianapolis, Brian Baldinger and Zefross Moss were the tackles, Pat Tomberlin and Randy Dixon the guards, and Ray Donaldson the center. Kevin Call will probably return to his old spot at RT, which would help. But the talent is just fair; and the depth, awful.

George (181 for 334, 2,152 yards, 16 TDs) had a spectacular rookie season and should be the Indy QB right into the next century — if he gets some protection. If veteran Jack Trudeau is healthy, he'll be the backup, with Mark Herrmann ready.

When he has time, George throws to exceptional Billy Brooks (62 catches for 823 yards) and surprising Jesse Hester (54 for 924). With Eugene Riley gone (Plan B to Detroit), Pat Beach and Orson Mobley will man the TEs. Neither is much of a receiver.

The future may be past for Colt RBs Eric Dickerson and Albert Bentley. Both are solid contributors, with Dickerson (166 for 677) providing the only speed. Bentley (137 for 556, 71 catches for 664) is a plodder.

The defensive line has almost as many problems as the offensive group. Ends Donnell Thompson (a disappointment) and Jon Hand and nose tackles Harvey Armstrong and Tony Siragusa are decent vs. the run, poor vs. the pass. Shane Curry, the top pick, should help the rush.

The linebackers are a notch better. Duane Bickett and Chip Banks man the outside. LILB Jeff Herrod is a top talent, but his running mates, Scott Radecic and expensive Fredd Young, haven't impressed.

The so-so secondary would be far better if the front seven applied more pressure. CBs Chris Goode and Eugene Daniel are fair; SS Keith Taylor and FS Mike Prior are marginally better.

The special teams are — surprise — wonderful! Return man Clarence Verdin is a Pro Bowler; kickers Rohn Stark and Dean Biasucci are outstanding.

AFC East
NEW ENGLAND PATRIOTS
1990 Finish: Fifth
1991 Prediction: Fifth

Brent Williams   **Tom Hodson**

If you don't include famous moments like
Pats' owner Victor Kiam apologizing and
apologizing, the New England 1990 high-
light video might run only four or five
minutes. The Pats somehow beat Indianapolis in the season's second game (a 16–
14 blowout), then lost 14 straight.

Enter new front-office boss Sam Janko-
vich and new head coach Dick McPherson.
If all the king's horses and men couldn't
help Humpty Dumpty, then Sam and Mac
have real problems.

Tommy Hodson (85 for 156, 968 yards, 4
TDs) probably gets the call at QB, with
untested Hugh Millen in the background.
Say good-bye to Mark Wilson and Steve
Grogan, possibly not a moment too soon.

RB John Stephens (212 carries for 808

yards) may still be one of the NFL's best, but he'll need more blocking than he got last year from FB Marvin Allen. First-round choice Leonard Russell fits in, but a decent offensive line would help, too.

LT Bruce Armstrong must be the best of a weak lot and is probably much better qualified to play at guard. So McPherson will sort out '90 starters Gs Damian Johnson and Chris Gambol, C Danny Villa, T Dave Viaene, top draft pick T Pat Harlow, and a cast of thousands — and then pray.

If Hodson gets a second or two to look for a receiver, he may be in luck. This is the Pats' most talented group, including Hart Lee Dykes (34 catches for 549 yards), Irving Fryar (54 for 856), and Greg McMurtry (22 for 240), once a first-round draft pick of the Red Sox. Underrated Marv Cook (51 for 455) is back at TE.

Actually, the picture on defense is much prettier. The line features ends Ray Agnew and Brent Williams, along with a healthy Garin Veris, plus NTs Tim Goad and Fred DeRiggi. Not bad. Linebacking is in fairly good shape, too, particularly if LOLB Andre Tippett, a former All-Pro, finally stays healthy, and ROLB Chris Singleton lives up to his advance billing. Ed Reynolds and Vincent Brown should return inside.

The secondary needs work. There's nobody to push vet LCB Ronnie Lippett, who should be back, along with RCB Maurice Hurst. SS Rod McSwain and FS Fred Marion have seen better days.

HOUSTON OILERS

1990 Finish: First (tied)
1991 Prediction: First

Warren Moon

Haywood Jeffires

Though Jerry Glanville is long gone, the Oilers still treat their Astrodome home as the House of Pain and the road like a house of horrors. Coach Jack Pardee's Oilers, even with their sometimes mind-blowing run-and-shoot offense, must still learn to play consistently and to win on the road.

QB Warren Moon, who led the NFL in just about everything (362 for 584, 33 TDs, 4,689 yards, despite a dislocated thumb in Week 15), makes the offense happen, and backup Cody Carlson showed that he can step in when needed, too. Both need a boost at wide receiver, though four Oilers managed 66 or more catches. The leader, Heywood Jeffires (74 for 1,048, 8 scores), should be there for years, but Drew Hill (74 for 1,019, 5 TDs) is beginning to show his age. Plan

Bs Richard L. Johnson and Cedric Jones will help. Ernest Givins (72 for 979, 9 scores) is first-rate. But the run-and-shoot requires seven or eight wideouts, and Houston seems a little short.

Up front, center is the major question mark. If All-Pro guard Bruce Matthews moves there permanently, Doug Dawson will join Mike Munchak at guard. If not, the Oilers will have to find a No. 1 center. Tackles Don Maggs and David Williams are adequate, though age is a problem.

Pardee would love to find a Thurman Thomas- or Barry Sanders-type back (tall order) to replace vets Lorenzo White (168 carries for 702 yards) and Alan Pinkett (66 for 268).

There's potential on the defensive front, where tackle Ray Childress is as good as it gets, and ends William Fuller and Sean Jones are returning from spectacular (for them) years. Jeff Alm and Willis Peguese have the tools to help soon. Meanwhile, tackle Doug Smith gets the call.

The development of former No. 1 draftee Lamar Lathon is the key to the linebacking corps. MLB Al Smith tries to improve on his best year, and RLB Johnny Meads is tops.

The secondary is a major weakness. Forget FS Terry Kinard. SS Bubba McDowell is especially strong vs. the run, and Richard Johnson is the best of the corners. The defensive backfield, a key to a possible AFC Central title in '91, was hit hard with Plan B losses, but draftee Mike Dumas helps.

AFC Central
PITTSBURGH STEELERS
1990 Finish: First (tied)
1991 Prediction: Second

David Little   **Louis Lipps**

This is a tough bunch to figure. QB Bobby Brister (223 of 387, 2,725 yards, 20 TDs) is beginning to get some respect, which he deserves. Now that he knows offensive coordinator Joe Walton's complicated system, '91 should be even better. Neil O'Donnell, an early '90 draft pick, should replace Rick Strom as Brister's backup. But Pittsburgh's passing game was last in the AFC a year ago and the questions persist.

The running game was a little better and should continue to improve. Merril Hoge is back for his third season as a starter, off career highs of 772 yards and 10 TDs. The key to improvement is Tim Worley, an '89 first-rounder, who has yet to stay healthy, physically or mentally. Warren Williams and Barry Foster back up.

Louis Lipps, the eight-year vet, remains the most dangerous Steeler receiver (50 catches for 682 yards). But how good would he be if head coach Chuck Noll can find another burner to play on the opposite side?

When 270-pound rookie TE Eric Green held out last year, Noll pronounced that 1990 would be a lost season for the hefty one. Then Green checked in, played 13 games, and merely led all NFL TEs in TDs with seven. Bookend tight end Mike Mularkey must bounce back from surgery.

With John Rienstra gone (Plan B to Cleveland), there's some room at guard where Brian Blankenship and Terry Long should hold forth. Tackles John Jackson and 12-year-vet Tunch Ilkin get the call at tackle with Dermontti Dawson in the pivot.

There's plenty of speed along the defensive front, including top pick DE Huey Richardson. Ends Keith Willis and Donald Evans sandwich NT Gerald Williams, with Aaron Jones ready to jump in.

The linebackers are solid, if not deep. A key is the development of quick OLB Jerrol Williams, now in his third year. Both OLB Bryan Hinkle and ILB David Little are beginning to show their age. Greg Lloyd is back on the outside.

The secondary is a big plus, led by All-Pro RCB Rod Woodson. SS Carnell Lake is a future Pro Bowler, LCB David Johnson is coming fast, and FS Thomas Everett is a big hitter out of the Ronnie Lott mold, which isn't too shabby.

AFC Central
CINCINNATI BENGALS

1990 Finish: First (tied)
1991 Prediction: Third

David Fulcher   **James Brooks**

The Bengals' team doctor will have to come up big for Sam Wyche's team to repeat atop the AFC Central in '91. The NFL's best tackle, Anthony Munoz, returns from a torn rotator cuff that kept him out against the Raiders last January. It was Munoz's first game absence ever. Since the powerful All-Pro makes everyone else on the line better, his good health is essential.

Guards Brian Blados and Bruce Reimers are both returning from injuries, too. But the Bengal line is solid, with C Bruce Kozerski and T Joe Walter joining Munoz, Blados, and Reimers. There's depth, too.

Good health is also key for QB Boomer Esiason (224 for 402, 3,031 yards, 24 TDs). Now 30 years old, the blond bomber threw only 18 times a game over the last six games of '90, when a sore arm limited him severely. With Plan B Todd Philcox off to Cleveland, only Eric Wilhelm is left to back up Boomer. It's a problem.

The healthy return of Ickey Woods (64 carries for 268 yards) and 32-year-old James Brooks (195 for 1,004) will assure the performance of a solid backfield. Look for Harold Green (83 for 353) to get even more playing time in '91.

The receiving corps, led by All-Pro TE Rodney Holman (40 for 596) and WRs Eddie Brown (44 for 706, 9 TDs) and Tim McGee (43 for 737), are only as good as Boomer's left arm makes them. Ex-Jet top draft Reggie Rembert, finally off IR, should make this group even better.

OLB James Francis (team-leading 78 tackles, eight sacks as a rookie in '90) was the surprise leader of the Cincy defense and should get better. His LB partners, Leon White outside and Carl Zander and Kevin Walker inside, are solid enough.

Up front, NT Tim Krumrie still isn't 100% after the broken leg he suffered in Super Bowl XXIII. Young vet DRE David Grant has his moments, but DLE Skip McClendon usually doesn't.

The secondary should be fine, if Cincy finally decides what to do with LCB Lewis Billups, a constant thorn in management's side. With Carl Carter and Rod Jones on hand to join RCB Eric Thomas, Billups could be dealt. David Fulcher and Barney Bussey should return at the safeties.

41

AFC Central
CLEVELAND BROWNS
1990 Finish: Fourth
1991 Prediction: Fourth

Michael Dean Perry   **Kevin Mack**

New Browns head coach Bill Belichick may be in for the shock of his life. The mentor of the Super Bowl-champion Giants defense gets his first shot at a head-coaching job. It may turn ugly before Bill can think about another Super Bowl trip.

The Browns, who broke every negative record in the Cleveland book in their 3–13 1990 season, dipped heavily into the Plan B pool in preparing for '91. It may help, but the Brownies have miles to go.

Bernie Kosar (230 for 423, 2,562 yards, 10 TDs) returns at QB, sidearm delivery and all. The running game is strange. FB Kevin Mack (158 for 702 yards, 5 TDs) was the team's toughest back a year ago, a shining light in an otherwise confused group. Terry Metcalf (80 for 248, plus 52 kickoff returns for 1,052 yards and 2 TDs) has scads of talent — which Belichick must channel. Leroy Hoard is talented, too, but not focused enough to succeed. Lawyer Tillman may move to TE to replace retired Ozzie Newsome. The old (too old?) crowd of Reggie Langhorne, Webster Slaughter, and Brian Brennan work the outside, along with younger Vernon Joines and Mike Oliphant.

A couple of Plan B pickups, ex-Steeler G John Rienstra and T Rob Woods, should help prevent a repeat of last year's disaster area up front. Look for Paul Ferren and Tony Jones to battle Woods, and Ralph Tamm and Gregg Rakoczy to challenge Rienstra. Once-retired C Mike Babb should be back.

If Cleveland switches to a 4–3 defense, they'll need another tackle to join Pro Bowler Michael Dean Perry. Two promising youngsters, Rob Burnett and Anthony Pleasant, will man the ends, along with Al Baker and Rhondy Weston. Linebacking could be in decent shape, with Clay Matthews, David Brandon, Richard Brown, David Grayson, and Eddie Johnson, though Johnson and Matthews are showing age.

Only four years ago, Cleveland's secondary was among the NFL's best. Now it's just one more area for Belichick to shore up, starting with top pick Eric Turner. Aged Ray Clayborn remains a solid corner, even at 36. Frank Minnifield is finished. At safety, Harlon Barnett and Thane Gash, with decent backups, aren't bad.

AFC West
LOS ANGELES RAIDERS
1990 Finish: First
1991 Prediction: First

Greg Townsend

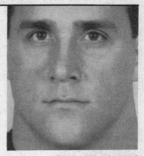

Steve Wisniewski

Can lightning possibly strike again? Raiders managing general partner Al Davis has made a career of saving aged souls. Over the years, when other teams have given up on "washed up" stars, the Raiders grabbed them and wound up wearing Super Bowl rings. Will history repeat with ex-49er heroes Roger Craig and Ronnie Lott? It should be fun finding out.

The Raiders don't need a heckuva lot of help. With Bo Jackson (125 carries for 698 yards in his usual half season) probably finished, the versatile Craig joins equally versatile Marcus Allen (179 for 682 yards, 12 TDs) and rookie Nick Bell in the L.A. backfield. One of last year's backups (Greg Bell or Steve Smith?) will be gone.

What's the verdict on QB Jay Schroeder

(182 for 334, 2,849 yards, 19 TDs)? We still can't tell. Superb in the play-off opener vs. Cincinnati, he was horrid in the Buffalo final. Held out through all of '91, Steve Beuerlein may be back, and top draft Todd Marinovich is on hand.

Any QB would be delighted to throw to the Raider wideouts. Willie Gault (50 catches for 985 yards), Mervyn Fernandez (52 for 839), Tim Brown (18 for 265), and company can run and catch. TEs Ethan Horton (33 for 404) and Mike Dyal are excellent receivers, fair blockers.

Guard-to-guard, the Raider offensive front is wonderful. C Don Mosebar plays between Gs Steve Wisniewski and Max Montoya, and all three are rock-solid. Not so with tackles Rory Graves and Steve Wright, though Graves is improved. Bruce Wilkerson gets a shot at Wright's spot.

A healthy Anthony Smith will push DEs Howie Long and Greg Townsend, who surround DTs Bob Golic and Scott Davis. It's a good group. The Raiders linebackers, on the other hand, are shaky. MLB Riki Ellison is 31, LLB Jerry Robinson is 34, and RLB Tom Benson is just so-so against the pass.

On the other hand, the secondary is absolutely marvelous. Lott should replace Mike Harden at SS, with Eddie Anderson returning at FS. LCB Terry McDaniel is nearing All-Pro status; RCB Lionel Washington is more than adequate; and DBs Garry Lewis, Torin Dorn, and Dan Land are coming fast.

AFC West
KANSAS CITY CHIEFS
1990 Finish: Second
1991 Prediction: Second

John Alt

Christian Okoye

It hasn't been long since the Kansas City Chiefs relied on their special teams to put points on the board. These days, coach Marty Schottenheimer has a scoring machine on board — though a key injury or two could hurt badly.

One tricky spot: quarterback. Steve DeBerg is talented, courageous — and 37. Steve actually had his best year (258 of 444 for 3,444 yards, 23 TDs, and only four interceptions) at age 36, so his fans are optimistic about age 37. If he goes down — and he won't go easily — ex-Charger Mark Vlasic and Steve Pelluer will challenge.

WR Stephone Paige (65 catches, 1,021 yards) does it all. On the other side, Kaycee hopes that Fred Jones or perhaps J.J. Birden becomes the breakaway threat to take the pressure off Paige. Blocking-oriented Jonathan Hayes will likely be back at TE, though ex-Ram Plan B Pete Holohan is a better receiver and Danta Whitaker is a better athlete.

The running game is in even better shape, particularly if Barry Word (204 for 1,015 yards) is the real thing. Hefty Christian Okoye still managed 805 yards on 245 carries. Kaycee is loaded with runners, but a contribution by Todd McNair or rookie Harvey Williams would help.

Pro Bowl LT John Alt is the key to an offensive line that features second-year men Dave Szott at left guard and Tim Grunhard at center. With vets David Lutz at RG and Rich Baldinger at RT, this unit is in great shape.

The starting defensive line — ends Neil Smith and Bill Maas and NT Dan Saleaumua — is excellent, though depth is a problem. Ex-Jet Ron Stallworth, if healthy, will help.

By himself, All-Pro ROLB Derrick Thomas makes the linebacker crew among the league's best. But there's plenty more with LOLB Chris Martin, LILB Percy Snow, and RILB Dino Hackett, though depth is a problem here, too.

Age is the only question in the secondary, where All-Pro LCB Albert Lewis is the group leader. Safeties Deron Cherry, injured late last season, and Lloyd Burruss have both been to Pro Bowls. SS Kevin Porter is first-rate.

AFC West
DENVER BRONCOS
1990 Finish: Fifth
1991 Prediction: Third

John Elway　　　　　　　　**Bobby Humphrey**

Sure, the Broncos just weren't in the same Super Bowl league with the NFC's best. But last in the AFC West? The disaster in Denver was amazing.

But this simply isn't a last-place team, and coach Dan Reeves and company should prove it in '91. If his back is healthy, QB John Elway (294 for 502, 3,526 yards, 15 TDs) remains one of the best clutch passers in the game. If the Broncos are in the hunt in the final minutes, Elway can frighten the opponents right out of their chin straps. If he goes down, however, there's a problem — because backup Gary Kubiak's back is in even worse shape.

RB Bobby Humphrey (288 carries for 1,202 yards, 7 TDs) is an exciting feature of a Denver offense that couldn't run at all before he arrived. There's a shortage at fullback, however. Sammy Winder retired, Steve Sewell is fragile, and Melvin Bratton is a disappointment.

If Elway's effectiveness slips, blame it on his receivers. Vance Jackson, Mark Jackson, Michael Young, and Rickey Nattiel aren't tough enough to pick up yardage on those occasions when they actually catch the football. And the tight end picture is worse. If Clarence Kay can stay out of trouble, that's great; otherwise, Denver will wait on top-notch rookie Reggie Johnson.

Darrell Hamilton and Ken Lanier should return at the tackles, unless problem child Gerald Perry somehow rallies. Ex-Cowboy G Crawford Ker joins Doug Widell, promising Jeff Davidson, and vets Jim Juriga and Sean Farrell at the guards. Keith Kartz starts his fifth year at center.

The defensive line is full of questions. Ends Warren Powers and Ron Holmes have disappointed, and Alphonso Carreker has been injured. In the middle, Greg Kragen and Andre Townsend are set.

ROLB Simon Fletcher is an excellent rusher, but LOLB Tim Lucas may give way to Jeff Mills or top pick Mike Croel. Karl Mecklenburg and Michael Brooks are back inside.

SS Dennis Smith and FS Steve Atwater are the secondary leaders. But neither LCB Randy Robbins nor RCB Wymon Henderson are championship caliber. The kicking game is in decent shape.

AFC West
SEATTLE SEAHAWKS
1990 Finish: Third
1991 Prediction: Fourth

Dave Krieg   **Brian Blades**

Man-for-man, there wasn't a single injured-reserve unit in the NFL that could touch the Seahawks injured-reserve unit in 1990. In the linebacker area alone, Seattle had six excellent players on the list. The secondary was wiped out, too. Examined carefully, Seattle's 9–7 record was a credit to hard work, courage, and a heavy dose of excellent coaching.

Take Nesby Glasgow, for example. Forced into the starting lineup in Game 4, the 33-year-old SS became the team's top tackler. A healthy Vann McElroy will probably start in '91, along with Eugene Robinson. It's the same at cornerback, where Brian Davis returns from the injured list to rejoin Patrick Hunter and Dwayne Harper.

Outside 'backers Dave Ahrens and Joe

Cain finished the season as starters with Dave Wyman in the middle. Seattle needs speed-rusher Rufus Porter to return from knee surgery and full recoveries by the rest of the crew.

DRT Cortez Kennedy missed 46 days of practice in '90, waiting for a contract he was satisfied with. He should become an impact player from Day 1 in '91. Aging DLE Jacob Green will try to match his 12.5 sacks, joining tackles Joe Nash and Jeff Bryant and LB-turned-end Tony Woods.

Dave Krieg (265 for 448, 3,194 yards, 15 TDs but 20 INTs) remains the QB of the present. The first-round pick of San Diego State's huge Dan McGwire may mean that Kelly Stouffer's days are numbered.

The running game is in capable hands, as long as RB Derrick Fenner (215 carries for 859 yards, 14 TDs) remains focused and FB John L. Williams (187 carries for 714 yards, 73 pass receptions for 699 yards) maintains his own high standards. WR Brian Blades (49 catches for 525 yards) is Seattle's most dangerous receiver, with help needed from late-blooming Tommy Kane (52 for 776). Another speedy receiver would help. TE Travis McNeal has shown flashes of brilliance and must do more.

Up front, RT Ronnie Lee and RG Bryan Millard have slipped badly, though LT Andy Heck is coming on. Edwin Bailey and Darrick Britz should battle for a spot at guard, with Grant Feasel and Joe Tofflemire providing strength at center.

SAN DIEGO CHARGERS
1990 Finish: Fourth
1991 Prediction: Fifth

Marion Butts

Leslie O'Neal

If Billy Joe Tolliver ever steps up and becomes a major-league quarterback and if personnel ace Bobby Beathard finds some companions for CB Gill Byrd, Sundays could become fun again in San Diego.

Tolliver (216 for 410, 2,574 yards, 16 TDs and 16 INTs) has a big-league arm but makes Little League mistakes too frequently. Untested John Friesz might be the answer someday and may get his chance.

RB Marion Butts (265 carries for 1,225 yards, 8 TDs), a 6'1", 248-pound cannonball, shocked more than a few NFL folks with his spectacular 1990. There's decent depth, too, with Rod Bernstine, Ronnie Harmon, and rookie Eric Bieniemy.

WR Anthony Miller (63 catches, 933 yards, 7 TDs) is a big-time weapon who'll be even better with a speedy running mate to reduce the pressure level. The TE picture is excellent, too, with Arthur Cox (14 for 93) the leader of a group that basically blocks and catches dump passes.

Coach Dan Henning has totally revamped the Charger offensive line, thanks in part to spectacular rookie seasons from C Frank Cornish and LT Leo Goeas. Veteran (well, a three-year man) Dave Richards returns at RG with Courtney Hall and possibly ex-Redskin Plan B Mark May on the opposite side. Broderick Thompson should pair with Goeas at T.

AFC quarterbacks aren't thrilled to see San Diego on their schedules. The Chargers pass-rush can be fearsome, led by LDE Lee Williams (7.5 sacks). Burt Grossman at RDE and NT Tony Savage are solid.

ROLB Leslie O'Neal (13.5 sacks), a two-time Pro Bowler, leads a capable quartet that was strengthened by a solid rookie performance by RILB Junior Seau. Longtime Charger Billy Ray Smith and Gary Plummer man the left side.

LCB Byrd (7 INTs) is the strength of a so-so secondary. Speedy RCB Sam Seale, a fine cover man, plays the opposite side. The problem area is safety, where SS Martin Bayless is looking for help. Anthony Shelton, Lester Lyles, and top draft pick Stanley Richard will get a shot.

Under coach Larry Pasquale, the Chargers' special teams were among the most improved in the league last year.

When you pick your All-Pro team, you start
at wide receiver with the Niners' Jerry Rice
— and then you go to work!

National
Football
Conference
Team Previews

NFC East
WASHINGTON REDSKINS
1990 Finish: Second (tied)
1991 Prediction: First

Ricky Sanders   **Mark Rypien**

Why is the NFC East the most competitive division in the league? No other division has the talent and depth of the East's Giants, Eagles, and Redskins.

Coach Joe Gibbs's team was better than last year's 10–6 record, with victories over the Bills and Eagles, and near misses against the Giants and Niners. A little nip here and a tuck there, and the 'Skins could have been in Tampa.

One of Gibbs's quarterbacks needs to step forward and prove he's No 1. Mark Rypien (166 of 304, 2,070 yards, and 16 TDs) figures to get the call. Stan Humphries (91 of 156, 1,015 yards, 3 TDs) has a super arm that gets wild at times. And young Cary Conklin could get a shot in '91. RB Earnest Byner (297 for 1,219 yards) returns from his best season, including 770 yards during the last eight weeks. Gerald Riggs (123 for 475) is an excellent partner, when healthy.

Washington uses loads of three-WR sets, so depth is a major factor. Art Monk (68 catches for 770 yards, 5 TDs) improves with age, but age is now a factor. Still, when Ricky Sanders slumped in '90, Gary Clark (75 for 1,112 and 8 TDs) was superb. TE Don Warren is getting on in years.

Though the remaining Hogs up front are aging, Washington seems to be prepared. C Jeff Bostic may have another season left, but LG Russ Grimm and RT Joe Jacoby may be ready to give way. The health of Ts Ed Simmons and Mo Elewonibi is a key to plans for '91. LT Jim Lachey is the NFL's best, and Gs Raleigh McKenzie and Mark Schlereth are first-rate.

A new outside rusher would be a major plus on the defensive front. Fred Stokes, a '90 Plan B pickup, was the leading sacker last year. Look for DT Tracy Rocker and top pick Bobby Wilson to push Tim Johnson and Darryl Grant. Charles Mann and Markus Koch should be back at DE.

Ex-Raider and 49er Matt Millen should bolster the Redskins at MLB, with Wilber Marshall and surprise rookie Andre Collins back on the outside.

The secondary is a problem. FS Todd Bowles is gone (Plan B to San Francisco), but ex-Eagle Terry Hoage should step in. SS Alvin Walton has lost a step. Only RCB Darrell Green keeps the backfield together.

NFC East
NEW YORK GIANTS
1990 Finish: First
1991 Prediction: Second

John Elliott

Jeff Hostetler

The Giants' off-season turmoil peaked on May 15. That's when coach Bill Parcells announced his departure after eight mostly up campaigns. That leaves new boss Ray Handley with high expectations, a revamped staff, possibly no Mark Bavaro, and a furious QB battle (Phil Simms vs. Super Bowl hero Jeff Hostetler).

Simms (184 for 311, 2,284 yards, 15 TDs) was enjoying perhaps his best season when he went down in mid-December. Hostetler (20 for 32, 222 yards, 1 TD in the big one in Tampa) has been patiently waiting his turn and may be patient no longer. Simms may be better; Hostetler is younger. Either way, it's time to groom a successor.

A healthy RB Rodney Hampton (109 for 455 yards, plus 20 kickoff returns for 17.0) should hold off aging Ottis Anderson, the Super Bowl MVP. Mo Carthon, strictly a blocker and now 30 years old, will feel the heat from 248-pound rookie Jarrod Bunch. Shifty David Meggett will see more action.

If Bavaro is done, the Giants have TE trouble. Howard Cross and Bob Mrosko are blockers, not receivers. The wide men, including Mark Ingram, Steven Baker, and Stacy Robinson, need help and depth (Plan B James Milling; draft pick Ed McCaffrey?).

Up front, the Giants are in super shape, led by Ts John (Jumbo) Elliott and Doug Riesenberg and Gs William Roberts and Eric Moore. If attorney C Bart Oates retires, Brian Williams is ready to step in.

The defensive front (DEs Eric Dorsey, Leonard Marshall, and Mike Fox; NT Erik Howard) are better against the run than the pass. They'll need to apply more pressure if OLB Lawrence Taylor shows signs of slipping. If not, he's back with the same great group of LBs — All-Pro ILB Pepper Johnson and running mate Gary Reasons, super OLB Carl Banks, backups Steve DeOssie and Johnnie Cooks, and No. 2 draftee Kanavis McGhee.

The secondary is loaded, with corners Mark Collins, Everson Walls, and Perry Williams, and safeties Myron Guyton, Greg Jackson, Adrian White, and Dave Duerson. The special teams are wonderful. Reyna Thompson is the game's No. 1 headhunter. Play-off hero PK Matt Bahr won't have to fight departed Raul Allegre for his job.

NFC East
PHILADELPHIA EAGLES
1990 Finish: Second
1991 Prediction: Third

Keith Byars   **Seth Joyner**

The king is dead, long live the new king. After five stormy years, Philadelphia Eagles coach Buddy Ryan was dismissed after a 20–6 loss to the Redskins in the opening round of the 1990 play-offs. The new man in the city without much brotherly love for losers is former offensive coordinator Rich Kotite. The hot seat is already warm.

Winning the NFC East, arguably the NFL's toughest division, won't be easy. But Kotite may well have the most talent in the bunch. Start with QB Randall Cunningham (271 for 465, 3,466 yards, NFC-high 30 TDs, plus a team-leading 942 yards rushing). Nobody does it better, though Randall tends to force the issue when the opportunities don't exist.

Versatile Keith Byars (81 catches for 819

yards) is a major pass-catching threat out of the backfield, with Heath Sherman (164 for 685 yards) and Anthony Toney (132 for 452) chewing up most of the non-Randall rushing yards.

Young WRs Calvin Williams (37 for 602, 9 TDs) and Fred Barnett (36 for 721, 8 TDs) give Philly outside strength for years to come. TE Keith Jackson (50 for 670, 6 TDs) is backed up by vet Mickey Shuler.

The offensive line is in good shape, with 330-pound rookie Antone Davis joining Gs Mike Schad and Ron Solt, Ts Reggie Singletary, Matt Darwin, and Ron Heller, and C Dave Alexander.

The defensive line may be the NFL's best. DE Reggie White (15 sacks) is a terror, possibly because DE Clyde Simmons and T Jerome Brown are so good. T Mike Pitts isn't in their class. LB Seth Joyner (127 tackles) returns from his best year, but Jessie Small was a disappointment. The linebacking corps could use some help.

The Eagles secondary was hit hard by three Plan B departures. If Ben Smith makes the adjustment at corner, he and Eric Allen will form a potent duo. Safety could be a problem spot with both Wes Hopkins and Andre Waters slipping.

With defensive coordinator Jeff Fisher leaving for the Rams, Kotite will start his new career with ex-Browns head man Bud Carson in charge of the defense. Philly can move the ball, but can they stop the opponents from doing it better?

NFC East
DALLAS COWBOYS
1990 Finish: Fourth
1991 Prediction: Fourth

Emmitt Smith   **Troy Aikman**

It didn't take the 'Pokes long to depart the NFC cellar and drive back toward the top of the league. Dallas was 7–7 and in the play-off hunt before losing their last two games in '90. And with a pile of rookies, led by No. 1 Russell Maryland and WR Alvin Harper, the future is even brighter.

Troy Aikman (226 of 399, 2,579 yards, 11 TDs) is the quarterback that coach Jimmy Johnson knew he could be. His backup? That one could leave Johnson scratching his immovable hair. With his first full training camp under his belt, last year's rookie sensation, Emmitt Smith (241 for 937 yards and 11 TDs), should get even better. If FB Alonzo Highsmith somehow bounces back to his old form, the running game will be in super shape.

TE Jay Novacek (59 for 657 yards) was a major surprise in '90. If last year's rookie WR Alexander Wright blossoms, he'll join Harper, Kelvin Martin, and Michael Irvin to give Aikman the targets he needs.

Up front, vet G Crawford Ker is gone (to Denver via Plan B), creating a momentary gap. But C Mark Stepnoski is much improved, RT Nate Newton is an awesome blocker, and LT Mark Tuinei is solid.

The defensive unit starts out fine and finishes weakly. The line is excellent. Ends Tony Tolbert and Daniel Stubbs make QBs miserable, especially with help from leader Jim Jeffcoat. At the tackles, hard-rushing Jimmie Jones and Maryland will push Dean Hamel and Danny Noonan.

The linebacker situation is slightly less positive. If OLB Ken Norton returns healthy, the picture is somewhat rosier. Middle man Eugene Lockhart, passed over in Plan B bidding, should return, with Jack Del Rio, an improved Jesse Solomon, and rookie Dixon Edwards.

The secondary, on the other hand, is a mess. One-time Viking Issiac Holt, obtained in the infamous Herschel Walker deal, is the best of the lot and he's not a Hall-of-Fame candidate. Safeties Ray Horton (the team leader in fumble recoveries) and James Washington (who's inconsistent) should improve. But there's a way to go.

Johnson has made many of the right moves in returning the once-hopeless Cowboys to the middle of the NFC pack.

NFC East
PHOENIX CARDINALS
1990 Finish: Fifth
1991 Prediction: Fifth

Ken Harvey

Johnny Johnson

Who could blame Cardinal coach Joe Bugel for tooting his own horn? Expected to contend for the first pick in the 1991 draft, the Cards actually won five games and contended into the last month of the season for a play-off berth. And with some fine young players on hand, particularly in the offensive backfield, Bugel might need to hire a brass band soon.

When top rookie pick Anthony Thompson failed to report to training camp, seventh-rounder Johnny Johnson stepped in and reeled off three 100-yard games, 926 for the season. When Johnson was slowed by injuries, Thompson took over and pulled off 136- and 96-yard efforts.

We're not convinced that QB Timm Rosenbach (237 of 437, 3,098 yards, and 16

TDs) is the QB of the future — but Bugel is! Rosenbach will be more effective if the Cards can find another speedy outside receiver. Vet Roy Green (53 catches for 797 yards) can still move, but he's not a burner anymore. Rookie Ricky Proehl (56 team-leading catches for 802) is a possession-type. Longtime WR J.T. Smith was released, meaning Ernie Jones sees more action. Walter Reeves returns at TE.

The Cards are pleased with their offensive front, though they'd better watch Ts Luis Sharpe and Tootie Robbins, both in that plus-30 age group. Still, the jobs remain theirs to lose. Derek Kennard and Lance Smith are back at guard, with Bill Lewis at center. It's a pretty good quintet.

Freddie Joe Nunn leads the defensive front, at least until Dexter Manley proves that he is still, well, Dexter Manley. DE Rod Saddler and NG Jim Wahler should get their starting jobs back, though top picks Eric Swann and Mike Jones are here.

Bugel is relatively pleased with his line-backers, led by ROLB Ken Harvey, off a spectacular year. LILB Garth Jax is just fine, but RILB Eric Hill and LOLB Anthony Bell must show more than they have.

The secondary might be a problem. SS Tim McDonald can play for anyone, but FS Lonnie Young probably can't. The Card corners, Cedric Mack and Jay Taylor, just get by.

The kicking game can use some help. Punter Tom Tupa can also back up at QB.

NFC Central
CHICAGO BEARS
1990 Finish: First
1991 Prediction: First

Neal Anderson

Mark Bortz

Mike Ditka, the Bear who went from grizzly to teddy and loved it, starts his 10th season as the Chicago head coach with another NFC Central title firmly tucked away and enormous concern about his club's age and health.

The Bears' long-raging quarterback battle was settled when Mike Tomczak bolted for Green Bay as a Plan B. That leaves the top job to mobile Jim Harbaugh (180 for 312, 2,178 yards, 10 TDs), with Peter Tom Willis, a better thrower, in reserve. The running-back tandem of Neal Anderson (260 for 1,078 yards, 10 TDs) and Brad Muster (141 for 664 yards, 6 TDs) is as talented as any in the Central, but there's little depth behind them.

The now easygoing Ditka could go even easier if Chicago found another speedy outside receiver. Meanwhile, the Bears are in decent shape with Wendell Davis (38 catches for 572 yards) and Ron Morris (31 for 437) as starters and Glen Kozlowski and Dennis Gentry as backups. James Thornton and Cap Boso form a fine one-two punch at tight end.

The Bears' biggest concerns are their two lines. The offensive group is smaller than Ditka likes and older than most. The unit has been together for the better part of seven seasons, an unusually long tenure for an offensive line. Look for top pick Stan Thomas to join Jim Covert and Keith Van Horne at the tackles, sandwiching guards Mark Bortz and Tom Thayer and center Jay Hilgenberg. Guard Kurt Becker and tackle John Wojciechowski furnish the depth.

The retirement of Dan Hampton and the tragic death of Fred Washington leave major gaps at DT, where Steve McMichael (knee surgery — again!) and Fridge Perry figure to start. A somewhat tamer Richard Dent and heralded Trace Armstrong are back at the ends, joined by ex-Dolphin Eric Kumerow.

If all-time MLB Mike Singletary packs it in after this season, Dante Jones had better get ready to take over. Ron Rivera and Jim Morrissey figure to start outside.

The return of RCB Lemuel Stinson from knee surgery is a major question in the secondary. All-Pro FS Mark Carrier should be a fixture for a decade, joined by SS Shaun Gayle and LCB Donnell Woolford.

NFC Central
MINNESOTA VIKINGS
1990 Finish: Second (tied)
1991 Prediction: Second

Cris Carter

Chris Doleman

It's a crucial year for the Vikings. The surprise team of 1990 — the surprise being that they were surprisingly awful almost every week; they'll need to improve big time in '91 to avoid a total rebuilding job in '92.

Start at quarterback. Wade Wilson (82 for 146, 9 TDs) has the better arm; Rich Gannon (182 for 349, 16 TDs) is more mobile. Neither is a future All-Pro. Expensive RB Herschel Walker (184 carries for 770 yards, 5 TDs, 966 yards on kickoff returns) is the key to the running game, with a healthy Rick Fenney (87 for 376) battling Alfred Anderson (59 for 207) for the fullback spot.

The Vikes need another speedy receiver, though Anthony Carter (70 catches for 1,008 yards, 8 TDs) remains a threat on every play, and Hassan Jones (51 for 810 yards, 7

TDs) is an ideal partner. Powerful Steve Jordan returns at tight end, with support from Brent Novoselsky. A youngster should be groomed to replace Jordan, who turns 31 at the end of the season.

Age is beginning to become a factor on the offensive line, too. LG Randall McDaniel is at the top of his game, with Todd Kalis on the opposite side. LT Gary Zimmerman is solid, but RT Tim Irwin is beginning to slip at age 33. Kirk Lowdermilk, who started the last 13 games at center, will again battle 34-year-old Chris Foote for the top spot.

The return of past All-Pro Keith Millard at DRT will be a major plus. Major knee surgery removed the 6'5", 263-pounder from the lineup in the fifth week of last season. If he's not ready, Henry Thomas will return. DLE Al Noga continues to impress NFL doubters, while DRE Chris Doleman remains a big-time star.

The retirement of MLB Scott Studwell hurts the Vikes in two ways — on the field and in the locker room. He'll be missed. Outside men Mike Merriweather and Mark Dusbabek are solid citizens.

The secondary, led by SS Joey Browner (7 INTs), the best in the game, isn't too shabby. CBs Reggie Rutland and Carl Lee are fine, thank you. But the Vikings haven't had a good FS for years. Returning starter Darrell Fullington gets the first shot, with Plan Bs Solomon Wilcots and ex-Brown star Felix Wright ready to step in.

NFC Central
GREEN BAY PACKERS
1990 Finish: Second (tied)
1991 Prediction: Third

Tim Harris

Sterling Sharpe

Turns out the Packers were doing it with mirrors. The 10–6 surprises of '89 slipped back to 6–10 in '90, and the bleeding may not have stopped.

If Don "$10 Million" Majkowski doesn't make it back from rotator-cuff surgery, the Pack may be forced to use Bear Plan B reject Mike Tomczak. Off Majik's '90 pre-injury performance, neither prospect is pretty.

The Pack's 85.6 yards per game rushing total was the lowest in the franchise's storied *history*. That's ugly. FB Michael Haddix led the sorry group of runners with a "spectacular" 311 yards. Hope for the future comes from disappointing rookie Darrell Thompson (76 carries for 264 yards) who finished the season strong.

Better news came from the receivers.

Sterling Sharpe had 67 catches for 1,105 yards, despite cracked ribs suffered at midseason. There's hope for speedy youngsters Jeff Query and Charles Wilson. Meanwhile, Perry Kemp and Clarence Weathers are excellent possession-type receivers. Ed West and Jackie Harris, who can go deep, form a fine TE tandem.

The offensive line, which allowed 62 sacks (including the one that ended Majkowski's season), should improve if coach Lindy Infante returns Ron Hallstrom and Rich Moran at the guards. (Both were '90 hold-outs and never regained their starting spots.) C James Campen was a pleasant surprise, but huge RT Tony Mandarich remains a huge flop. LT Ken Ruettgers can do better than in '90.

The defensive line isn't much better. Ends Matt Brock and Robert Brown should again sandwich NT Bob Nelson, with talented Shawn Patterson ready to step in. ROLB Tim Harris is the leader of a terrific lineback-ing crew. Inside men Brian Noble and Tim Holland are beginning to show their age. Green Bay needs OLB Tony Bennett to ful-fill his pass-rushing potential.

The secondary has gone beyond "show-ing age" and has become downright old. RCB Jerry Holmes, SS Mark Murphy, and LCB Mark Lee are just about ready for Social Security. Fortunately, they can still play football. RCB LeRoy Butler is coming on strong, and FS Tiger Greene holds things together when Chuck Cecil doesn't.

NFC Central
DETROIT LIONS
1990 Finish: Second (tied)
1991 Prediction: Fourth

William White   **Rodney Peete**

After seven straight losing seasons, 6–10 shouldn't shock anyone in Detroit. But the Lions and their fans expected better in '90 — and it didn't happen. It may not happen in '91, though the offense should continue to terrify opponents and entertain spectators.

Coach Wayne Fontes may install new plays for RB Barry Sanders, perhaps the most explosive back in the NFL. With assistant coach Mouse Davis off to the new WLAF, the Lions may reduce their use of the run and shoot, which should get Sanders even more action. What if Barry gets hurt? Detroit doesn't even want to think about it.

Mobile Rodney Peete seems like a sure bet at QB, unless Andre Ware does something spectacular to change Fontes's mind.

Their wide receivers, including Robert Clark, Jeff Campbell, Mike Farr, and Terry Greer, aren't big enough, fast enough, and steady enough for the Lions' passing game. But for the most part, they'll have to do. Top draftee Herman Moore should make an impact.

The line is reasonably set, with guards Eric Andolsek, Ken Dallafior, and Mike Utley; All-Pro type Lomas Brown and former All-Pro Harvey Salem at tackle; and Kevin Glover at center. Glover may be the weakest link in the group.

What does the Detroit defensive line need to improve? "A guy who can blot out the sun," says Fontes. Failing that, the Lions will probably turn to a 4–3 scheme this fall, with top LB-rusher Mike Cofer moving to end. Among the returnees, NT Jerry Ball is the best QB-chaser. But his frequent holdouts and weight-gains have soured Detroit management. Keith Ferguson and Dan Owens, the returning ends, will find work.

If Cofer moves up front, young OLB Tracy Hayworth may become the new rushing threat. Chris Spielman, Victor Jones, and George Jamison should see plenty of action.

The secondary has tons of questions, including the possible return of CB Terry Taylor from the suspended list. Two Plan B pickups, Melvin Jenkins and Sean Vanhorse, will battle last year's starters, Ray Crockett and LeRoy Irvin, at the corners. FS Bennie Blades and SS William White get help from ex-Giant Herb Welch.

TAMPA BAY BUCCANEERS
1990 Finish: Second (tied)
1991 Prediction: Fifth

Mark Carrier

Wayne Haddix

The Tampa Bay Bucs lost seven players via Plan B free agency. Why would everyone want Bucs rejects? It's just one more unanswered question for a franchise with a history of questions.

Richard Williamson, who took over in December when head coach Ray Perkins was fired, gets a full shot in '91 with the youngest team in the NFL — but with a substantially upgraded schedule.

QB Vinny Testaverde (203 for 365, 2,818 yards, 17 TDs, 18 INTs) will probably get one more shot to prove that he is the real thing. Chris Chandler will wait again.

A new fullback is on the horizon. Last year's combo of Reggie Cobb (151 for 480 yards) and Gary Anderson (166 for 646) will be competing for one spot at RB. With a full camp behind him (he held out last year), WR Mark Carrier (49 catches for 813 yards) should be better. Partner Bruce Hill (42 for 641) showed outstanding potential in '90. TE Ron Hall may be the Central's best, with Jesse Anderson ready to back up.

Up front, youth will be served. Gs Ian Beckles and Tom McHale look like future stars, and C Tony Mayberry may be set to replace Randy Grimes. Huge top rookie Charles McRae joins Paul Gruber at T.

The picture on the defensive line is clouded. With hard work, Reuben Davis has a wonderful future. NT Jim Skow, an ex-Bengal, does the work but lacks the size.

New defensive coordinator Floyd Peters will switch the Bucs from a 3–4 to 4–3 alignment, which may force unfulfilled stars Broderick Thomas and Keith McCants from LB to DE. Kevin Murphy should be around for a while, and the Bucs will be well off with inside 'backers Eugene Marve, Winston Moss, and Ervin Randle.

The fact that safeties Harry Hamilton and Mark Robinson were Tampa Bay's leading tacklers last year (119 and 115, respectively) tells you everything you need to know about the Bucs defense. Look for Ricky Reynolds and Eric Everett to return on the corners, along with Pro Bowler Wayne Haddix (seven interceptions, three TDs), though anything is possible.

The kicking game may be the Bucs' best feature. PK Steve Christie and P Mark Royals were consistent all season.

NFC West
SAN FRANCISCO 49ERS
1990 Finish: First
1991 Prediction: First

John Taylor

Guy McIntyre

A not-so-funny thing happened to the San Francisco 49ers on their way to a three-peat in Super Bowl XXV. Giant Matt Bahr's last-second field goal derailed the Niner express, and now doubters are beginning to cast a wary eye. It's too soon.

Yes, there are some concerns, most of them minor. With Roger Craig off to the Raiders (Plan B), is Dexter Carter (114 carries for 460 yards) durable enough to join Tom Rathman (101 for 318) to power the already so-so running game? With intense, hard-hitting Ronnie Lott also gone to the Raiders, are Chet Brooks and Dave Waymer (both unprotected after the '90 season) good enough to get it done? Are the aging nose tackles (Michael Carter, Pete Kugler, Jim Burt) going to hold up all season?

But there's talent aplenty, starting at QB, where Joe Montana (321 for 520, 3,944 yards, 26 TDs), recovered from Giants end Leonard Marshall's visit last January, should again be in top form. If not, Steve Young (38 for 62, 427 yards) is football's best backup. Their receivers, led by the very best (ever?) Jerry Rice (league-leading 100 catches, 1,502 yards, 13 TDs), are merely fabulous. On any other team, John Taylor (49 for 748) is a superstar. A healthy Mike Sherrard can terrorize the best defensive backs. Brent Jones leads three capable tight ends.

LT Bubba Paris, overweight and immobile in '90, is becoming the weak link in an otherwise splendid offensive line. RT Steve Wallace, LG Guy McIntyre, RG Harris Barton, and C Jesse Sapolu are in control.

The defensive front remains a San Francisco plus, if the nosemen hold up. Ends Pierce Holt, Kevin Fagan, and Dennis Brown provide excellent pressure. All-Pro LOLB Charles Haley keys a linebacker corps that may miss LILB Matt Millen (Plan B to Washington). ROLB Bill Romanowski is solid, and Keith DeLong replaces Millen.

The defection by Lott could produce coach George Seifert's biggest problem. A leader on and off the field, Lott held the secondary together. Two unprotected safeties, aging Dave Waymer and Chet Brooks, might be on their own. Help may come from Plan Bs Todd Bowles (Washington) and David Whitmore (Giants). Darryl Pollard and Don Griffin will do well at the corners.

NFC West
LOS ANGELES RAMS

1990 Finish: Third (tied)
1991 Prediction: Second

Henry Ellard

Kevin Greene

It was sort of sad watching the Rams last season. After making the play-offs during six of coach John Robinson's first seven years at the helm, the Anaheim machine became the gang that couldn't shoot straight. There seems to be too much talent around for L.A. to flounder again in '91, but there are loads of concerns.

Jim Everett (307 of 554, 3,989 yards, 23 TDs) is set at QB, with Ram fans waiting for him to deliver on his All-World potential. Chuck Long backs up, but only in emergencies.

The running game is a major problem. Big gun Cleveland Gary (204 carries for 808 yards) has the nasty habit of putting the ball on the ground too often. If you believe in miracles, Marcus DuPree will take over in '91 and gain 1,000 yards. It would help.

Everett's receivers may be the best group in the league. Henry Ellard (76 catches for 1,294 yards) continues to amaze, and Flipper Anderson (51 for 1,097), Arthur Cox, and Derrick Faison can play for anyone. With Pete Holohan off to Kansas City (Plan B), TE Damone Johnson must crank it up.

The Ram offensive line continues to defy old age, but you must believe Robinson is watching his graybeards carefully. Tackles Jackie Slater and Irv Pankey, while still solid, have celebrated 68 birthdays between them. C Doug Smith may give way this time around, either to '90 rookie Bern Brostek or to frequent Pro Bowl G Tom Newberry. Either way, Duval Love has one guard position sewn up.

New defensive coordinator Jeff Fischer plans to have the Rams in a 4–3 set in '91, with fierce Kevin Greene moving to DE from LOLB. L.A. is set with tackles like Doug Reed, Alvin Wright, and Mike Piel. But ends may prove a difficult challenge.

With OLBs Mike Wilcher and Mel Owens having lost a step or so, it's more important than ever that Fred Strickland and Frank Stams put together healthy seasons.

Notre Dame stickout CB Todd Lyght should join vet Jerry Gray, who can get it done, though he's slipped a bit. The picture is much brighter at safety with Michael Stewart, Anthony Newman, and Pat Terrell.

The Rams should be better, but how much better is anyone's guess.

NFC West
NEW ORLEANS SAINTS
1990 Finish: Second
1991 Prediction: Third

Dalton Hilliard

Vaughan Johnson

Just when everyone in the NFL had written the '90 Saints off, coach Jim Mora's troops rallied from a 2–5 start to an 8–8 finish and a berth in the NFC play-offs. Thus spoiled, Saints fans will enter the '91 campaign expecting Mora the same!

Neither early-season starter John Fourcade nor late-season starter Steve Walsh proved to be the quarterback that '90 holdout Bobby Hebert was. Stay tuned for further developments. The running game should be solid, particularly if Dalton Hilliard (knee injury, sixth game) is sound. (He did return for the play-offs.) He'll be joined by Craig Heyward (a team-leading 599 yards on a 4.6 yard average), Rueben Mayes (7 TDs), and '90 rookie Gill Fenerty, a tough runner and fine receiver.

The receiving department is led by Eric Martin, a starter for anyone in the league. But among the rest of the crowd, including starter Brett Perriman, Floyd Turner, Lonzell Hill, and even Plan B pickups Quinn Early and Pat Newman, there isn't a burner in the bunch. Both TEs, Hoby Brenner and John Tice, have passed age 30.

The offensive front is solid and comes off a healthy year. There's a minor concern about RT Stan Brock's age, but LT Kevin Haverdink, Gs Jim Dombrowski and Steve Trapilo, and C Joel Hilgenberg form an excellent unit. Mora will eventually have to find some way to groom backups.

NT Robert Goff was a pleasant surprise in the middle last season. Jim Wilks, Renaldo Turnbull, and Wayne Martin should man the ends in '91. Watch for the possible return of Frank Warren, which would be a big bonus for the Saints.

The starting linebackers are first-rate. Rickey Jackson and headhunter Pat Swilling on the outside and Sam Mills and Vaughan Johnson on the inside form one of the NFL's premier foursomes. The only question about the LB crew is depth.

Youngster Vince Buck looks like he's ready to push Robert Massey and Toi Cook for a start on the corner. Safeties Brett Maxie and Gene Atkins are adequate for now.

The kicking game, led by the superior PK Morten Andersen, is in lovely shape. Those miserable days of the 'Aints are over for sure. These Saints are for real.

NFC West
ATLANTA FALCONS
1990 Finish: Third (tied)
1991 Prediction: Fourth

Mike Kenn   **Deion Sanders**

The wild, wacky world of the Man in Black, head coach Jerry Glanville, brought more than just a couple of extra victories to Atlanta last fall. He also brought hope, something that has been missing in the Georgia capital since the last Falcon play-off team, way back in 1982.

"We made a lot of progress on our long-term goals," said Glanville. "Nobody takes Atlanta for granted anymore."

Still, Glanville will be fortunate to last long enough — he generally wears out his welcome in a few years — to see Atlanta in its first Super Bowl. QB Chris Miller was enjoying his best season (222 of 388, 2,735 yards, 17 TDs) before a broken collarbone ended his season in Week 13. Glanville can't be too happy with Miller's backups,

Scott Campbell and Gilbert Renfroe.

Atlanta's red gun offense is perfectly suited to Miller and All-Pro WR Andre Rison (82 catches for 1,208 yards, 10 TDs). With frequent use of a four-receiver set, the Falcons need big contributions from Michael Haynes, Shawn Collins, Floyd Dixon, and first-rounder Mike Pritchard. RB Mike Rozier (153 carries for 675 yards) was a pleasant surprise after joining Atlanta on October 3, though he still fumbles too much and can't catch the ball. RBs Keith Jones and Steve Broussard should return.

The offensive line is much improved, though T Mike Kenn is 35 and may fade after a brilliant '90. Four-time Pro Bowler G Bill Fralic and T Chris Hinton should continue to anchor the line, though C Jamie Dukes is suspect.

Defensively, DEs Tim Green and Mike Gann return from their best years, with Tory Epps and Tony Casillas in the middle. ROLB Darion Conner leads a respectable group, especially if Aundray Bruce ever plays like a No. 1 draft pick. Meanwhile, Glanville favorite Robert Epps should start at LOLB, with Jessie Tuggle and a hopefully healthy John Rade in the middle.

At CB, Atlanta has ex-Niner and Dolphin Tim McKyer and top pick Bruce Pickens to go with Deion Sanders, who returned INTs for 82- and 61-yard TDs last season. But SS Brian Jordan (193 tackles) and FS Scott Case (170 tackles) are the guys who make this secondary go.

With All-Pro T Jim Lachey protecting QBs and blasting holes for the runners, the Redskins will be in the NFC East hunt.

1991
NFL
Draft List

The following abbreviations are used to identify the players' positions:

OFFENSE:
T = tackle; G = guard; C = center;
QB = quarterback; RB = running back;
WR = wide receiver; TE = tight end.

DEFENSE:
DE = defensive end; LB = linebacker;
DT = defensive tackle;
DB = defensive back.

SPECIAL TEAMS:
P = punter; K = placekicker.

The number before each player's name indicates the overall position in which he was drafted.

Atlanta Falcons
3. Bruce Pickens, DB, Nebraska; 13. Mike Pritchard, WR, Colorado; 33. Brett Favre, QB, So. Mississippi; 87. Moe Gardner, DT, Illinois; 114. James Goode, LB, Oklahoma; 145. Eric Pegram, RB, No. Texas St.; 172. Brian Mitchell, DB, Brigham Young; 186. Mark Tucker, C, USC; 199. Randy Austin, TE, UCLA; 226. Ernie Logan, DE, E. Carolina; 256. Walter Sutton, WR, SW Minnesota St.; 258. Peter Lucas, T, Wisconsin-Stevens Point; 283. Joe Sims, NT, Nebraska; 310. Robert Christian, RB, Northwestern.

Buffalo Bills

26. Henry Jones, DB, Illinois; Phil Hansen, DE, No. Dakota St.; 82. Darryl Wren, DB, Pittsburg (KS) St.; 138. Shawn Wilbourn, DB, Long Beach St.; 166. Millard Hamilton, WR, Clark (GA); 194. Amir Rasul, RB, Florida A&M; 222. Brad Lamb, WR, Anderson (IN); 249. Mark Maddox, LB, No. Michigan; 277. Tony DeLorenzo, G, New Mexico St.; 305. Dean Kirkland, G, Washington; 333. Stephen Clark, TE, Texas.

Chicago Bears

22. Stan Thomas, T, Texas; 49. Chris Zorich, DT, Notre Dame; 78. Chris Gardocki, P-K, Clemson; 105. Joe Johnson, DB, N.C. State; 134. Anthony Morgan, WR, Tennessee; 161. Darren Lewis, RB, Texas A&M; 190. Paul Justin, QB, Arizona St.; 217. Larry Horton, DB, Texas A&M; 245. Mike Stonebreaker, LB, Notre Dame; 272. Tom Backes, DE, Oklahoma; 301. Stacey Long, G, Clemson; 328. John Cook, DT, Washington.

Cincinnati Bengals

18. Alfred Williams, LB, Colorado; 46. Lamar Rodgers, DT, Auburn; 64. Bob Dahl, DE, Notre Dame; 99. Donald Hollas, QB, Rice; 109. Rob Carpenter, WR, Syracuse; 130. Mike Arthur, C, Texas A&M; 157. Richard Fain, DB, Florida; 184. Fernandous Vinson, DB, N.C. State; 211. Mike Dingle, RB, S. Carolina; 241. Shane Garrett, WR, Texas A&M; 268. Jim Lavin, G, Georgia Tech; 295. Chris Smith, TE, Brigham Young; 322. Antoine Bennett, DB, Florida A&M.

Cleveland Browns

2. Eric Turner, DB, UCLA; 29. Ed King, G, Auburn; 57. James Jones, DT, Iowa; 85. Pio Sagapolutele, DE, San Diego St.; 141. Michael Jackson, WR, So. Mississippi; 197. Frank Conover, DT, Syracuse; 225. Raymond Irvin, DB, Central Florida; 239. Shawn Wiggins, WR, Wyoming; 252. Brian Greenfield, P, Pittsburgh; 280. Todd Jones, G, Henderson St.; 308. Elijah Austin, DE, N.C. State.

Dallas Cowboys

1. Russell Maryland, DT, Miami; 12. Alvin Harper, WR, Tennessee; 37. Dixon Edwards, LB, Michigan St.; 63. Godfrey Myles, LB, Florida; 64. James Richards, G, California; 70. Erik Williams, T, Central State (OH); 97. Curvin Richards, RB, Pittsburgh; 106. Bill Musgrave, QB, Oregon; 108. Tony Hill, DE, Tennessee-Chattanooga; 110. Kevin Harris, DE, Texas Southern; 132. Darrick Brownlow, LB, Illinois; 153. Mike Sullivan, G, Miami; 173. Leon Lett, DT, Emporia St.; 235. Damon Mays, WR, Missouri; 264. Sean Love, G, Penn St.; 291. Tony Boles, RB, Michigan; 320. Larry Brown, DB, TCU.

Denver Broncos

4. Mike Croel, LB, Nebraska; 30. Reggie Johnson, TE, Florida St.; 61. Keith Traylor, LB, Central Oklahoma St.; 89. Derek Russell, WR, Arkansas; 115. Greg Lewis, RB, Washington; 142. Nick Subis, T, San Diego St.; 200. Kenny Walker, DE, Nebraska; 227. Don Gibson, NT, USC; 253. Curtis Mayfield, WR, Oklahoma St.; 284. Shawn Moore, QB, Virginia.

Detroit Lions

10. Herman Moore, WR, Virginia; 20. Kelvin Pritchett, DT, Mississippi; 58. Reggie Barrett, WR, Texas-El Paso; 91. Kevin Scott, DB, Stanford; 118. Scott Conover, G, Purdue; 151. Richie Andrews, K, Florida St.; 178. Franklin Thomas, TE, Grambling; 205. Cedric Jackson, RB, TCU; 231. Darryl Milburn, DE, Grambling; 285. Slip Watkins, WR, LSU; 318. Zeno Alexander, LB, Arizona.

Green Bay Packers

19. Vince Clark, DB, Ohio St.; 35. Esera Tuaolo, DT, Oregon St.; 67. Don Davey, DE, Wisconsin; 81. Chuck Webb, RB, Tennessee; 135. Jeff Fite, P, Memphis St.; 149. Walter Dean, RB, Grambling; 164. Joe Garten, C, Colorado; 169. Frank Blevins, LB, Oklahoma; 176. Reggie Burnette, LB, Houston; 203. Johnny Walker, WR, Texas; 229. Dean Witkowski, LB, N. Dakota; 262. Rapier Porter, TE, Arkansas-Pine Bluff; 289. J.J. Wierenga, WR, Johnson C. Smith.

Houston Oilers

28. Mike Dumas, DB, Indiana; 38. Darryl Lewis, DB, Arizona St.; 44. John Flannery, C, Syracuse; 71. Steve Jackson, DB, Purdue; 79. Kevin Donnalley, T, No. Carolina; 101. David Rocker, DT, Auburn; 102. Marcus Robertson, DB, Iowa St.; 129. Gary Wellman, WR, USC; 183. Kyle Freeman, LB, Angelo St.; 214. Gary Brown, RB, Penn St.; 240. Shawn Jefferson, WR, Cen. Florida; 267. Curtis Moore, LB, Kansas; 294. James Smith, DB, Richmond; 325. Alex Johnson, WR, Miami.

Indianapolis Colts

40. Shane Curry, DT, Miami; 69. Dave McCloughan, DB, Colorado; 96. Mark VanderPoel, T, Colorado; 125. Kerry Cash, TE, Texas; 152. Mel Agee, DT, Illinois; 181. James Bradley, WR, Michigan St.; 208. Tim Bruton, TE, Missouri; 236. Howard Griffith, RB, Illinois; 263. Frank Gianetti, DE, Penn St.; 292. Jerry Crafts, T, Louisville; 319. Rob Luedeke, C, Penn St.

Kansas City Chiefs

21. Harvey Williams, RB, LSU; 50. Joe Valerio, T, Penn; 77. Tim Barnett, WR, Jackson St.; 133. Charles Mincy, DB, Washington; 162. Darrell Malone, DB, Jacksonville St.; 189. Bernard Ellison, DB, Nevada; 218. Tim Dohring, T, Michigan; 244. Robbie Keen, K, California; 273. Eric Ramsey, DB, Auburn; 300. Bobby Olive, WR, Ohio St.; 329. Ron Shipley, G, New Mexico.

Los Angeles Raiders

24. Todd Marinovich, QB, USC; 43. Nick Bell, RB, Iowa; 100. Raghib Ismail, WR, Notre Dame; 146. Nolan Harrison, DT, Indiana; 213. Brian Jones, LB, Texas; 219. Todd Woulard, LB, Alabama A&M; 247. Tahaun Lewis, DB, Nebraska; 274. Andrews Glover, TE, Grambling; 330. Dennis Johnson, WR, Winston-Salem.

Los Angeles Rams

5. Todd Lyght, DB, Notre Dame; 31. Roman Phifer, LB, UCLA; 107. Robert Bailey, DB, Miami; 116. Robert Young, DT, Mississippi St.; 143. Neal Fort, T, Brigham Young; 170. Tyron Shelton, RB, William & Mary; 201.

Pat Tyrance, LB, Nebraska; 228. Jeff Fields, DT, Arkansas St.; 281. Terry Crews, LB, We. Michigan; 311. Jeff Pahukoa, T, Washington; 312. Ernie Thompson, RB, Indiana.

Miami Dolphins

23. Randal Hill, WR, Miami; 60. Aaron Craver, RB, Fresno St.; 113. Brian Cox, LB, We. Illinois; 121. Eugene Williams, G, Iowa St.; 191. Chris Green, DB, Illinois; 220. Roland Smith, DB, Miami; 246. Scott Miller, WR, UCLA; 275. Michael Titley, TE, Iowa; 302. Ernie Rogers, G, California; 331. Joe Bruncon, DT, Tennessee-Chattanooga.

Minnesota Vikings

65. Carlos Jenkins, LB, Michigan St.; 68. Jake Reed, WR, Grambling; 92. Randy Baldwin, RB, Mississippi; 119. Chris Thorne, C, Minnesota; 163. Todd Scott, CB, SW Louisiana; 179. Scott Reagan, DT, Humboldt St.; 180. Tripp Welborne, DB, Michigan; 206. Reggie Johnson, DE, Arizona; 232. Gerald Hudson, RB, Oklahoma St.; 259. Brady Pierce, T, Wisconsin; 286. Ivan Caesar, LB, Boston College; 313. Darren Hughes, WR, Carson-Newman.

New England Patriots

11. Pat Harlow, T, USC; 14. Leonard Russell, RB, Arizona St.; 41. Jerome Henderson, DB, Clemson; 56. Calvin Stephens, G, So. Carolina; 84. Scott Zolak, QB, Maryland; 112. Jon Vaughn, RB, Michigan; 124. Ben Coates, TE, Livingston; 140. Dave Key, DB, Michigan; 168. Blake Miller, C, LSU; 196. Harry Colon, DB, Missouri; 251. Randy Bethel, TE, Miami; 279. Vince Moore, WR, Tennessee; 303. Paul Alsbury, P, SW Texas St.; 307. Tim Edwards, DT, Delta St.

New Orleans Saints

42. Wesley Carroll, WR, Miami; 126. Reggie Jones, DB, Memphis St.; 154. Fred McAfee, RB, Mississippi College; 182. Hayward Haynes, G, Florida St.; 210. Frank Wainright, TE, No. Colorado; 237. Anthony Wallace, RB, California; 293. Scott Ross, LB, USC; 321. Mark Drabczak, G, Minnesota.

New York Giants

27. Jarrod Bunch, RB, Michigan; 55. Kanavis McGhee, LB, Colorado; 83. Ed McCaffrey, WR, Stanford; 114. Clarence Jones, T, Maryland; 139. Tony Moss, LB, Florida St.; 167. Corey Miller, LB, S. Carolina; 195. Simmie Carter, DB, So. Mississippi; 223. Lamar McGriggs, DB, We. Illinois; 250. Jerry Bouldin, WR, Mississippi St.; 278. Luis Cristobal, G, Miami; 306. Ted Poson, TE, Portland St.; 334. Larry Wanke, QB, John Carroll.

New York Jets

34. Browning Nagle, QB, Louisville; 62. Morris Lewis, LB, Georgia; 94. Mark Gunn, DT, Pittsburgh; 148. Blaise Bryant, RB, Iowa St.; 160. Mike Riley, DB, Tulane; 175. Doug Parrish, DB, San Francisco St.; 202. Tim James, DB, Colorado; 234. Paul Glonek, DT, Arizona; 261. Al Baker, RB, Kentucky; 288. Rocen Keeton, LB, UCLA; 315. Mark Hayes, T, Arizona St.

Philadelphia Eagles

8. Antone Davis, T, Tennessee; 48. Jesse Campbell, DB, N.C. State; 75. Rob Selby, T, Auburn; 104. William Thomas, LB, Texas A&M; 131. Craig Erickson, QB, Miami; 156. Andrew Harmon, DB, Kent St.; 187. James Joseph, RB, Auburn; 216. Scott Kowalkowski, LB, Notre Dame; 242. Chuck Weatherspoon, RB, Houston; 271. Eric Harmon, G, Clemson; 298. Mike Flores, DE, Louisville; 327. Darrell Beavers, LB, Morehead St.

Phoenix Cardinals

6. Eric Swann, DE, Bay State Titans; 32. Mike Jones, DE, N.C. State; 59. Aneas Williams, DB, Southern; 86. Dexter Davis, DB, Clemson; 117. Vance Hammond, DT, Clemson; 144. Eduardo Vega, T, Memphis St.; 171. Ivory Lee Brown, RB, Arkansas-Pine Bluff; 198. Greg Amsler, RB, Tennessee; 204. Jerry Evans, TE, Toledo; 209. Scott Evans, DT, Oklahoma; 255. Herbie Anderson, DB, Texas A&I; 282. Nathan LaDuke, DB, Arizona St.; 309. Jeff Bridewell, QB, Cal-Davis.

Pittsburgh Steelers

15. Huey Richardson, DE, Florida; 46. Jeff Graham, WR, Ohio St.; 73. Ernie Mills, WR, Florida; 88. Sammy Walker, DB, Texas Tech; 103. Adrian Cooper, TE, Oklahoma; 158. Leroy Thompson, RB, Penn St.; 185. Andre Jones, LB, Notre Dame; 212. Dean Dingman, G, Michigan; 239. Bruce McGonnigal, TE, Virginia; 269. Ariel Solomon, T, Colorado; 296. Efrum Thomas, DB, Alabama; 323. Jeff Brady, LB, Kentucky.

San Diego Chargers

9. Stanley Richard, DB, Texas; 36. George Thornton, DT, Alabama; 39. Eric Bieniemy, RB, Colorado; 47. Eric Moten, G, Michigan St.; 90. Yancey Thigpen, WR, Winston-Salem; 123. Duane Young, TE, Michigan St.; 127. Floyd Fields, DB, Arizona St.; 150. Jimmy Laister, T, Oregon Tech; 177. David Jones, WR, Delaware St.; 192. Terry Beauford, T, Florida A&M; 230. Andy Katoa, LB, So. Oregon; 254. Roland Poles, RB, Tennessee; 257. Mike Heldt, C, Notre Dame; 290. Joaquim Weinberg, WR, Johnson C. Smith; 317. Chris Samuels, RB, Texas.

San Francisco 49ers

25. Ted Washington, DE, Louisville; 45. Ricky Watters, RB, Notre Dame; 53. John Johnson, LB, Clemson; 95. Mitch Donahue, LB, Wyoming; 122. Merton Hanks, DB, Iowa; 137. Harry Boatswain, T, New Haven; 165. Scott Bowles, T, N. Texas; 193. Shedlon Canley, RB, San Jose St.; 221. Tony Hargain, WR, Oregon; 248. Louis Riddick, DB, Pittsburgh; 276. Byron Holdbrooks, DL, Alabama; 304. Bobby Slaughter, WR, Louisiana Tech; 314. Al Chamblee, LB, Louisiana Tech.

Seattle Seahawks

16. Dan McGwire, QB, San Diego St.; 51. Doug Thomas, WR, Clemson; 74. David Daniels, QB, Penn St.; 98. John Kasay, K, Georgia; 128. Harlan Davis, DB, Tennessee; 155. Mike Sinclair, DE, Ea. New Mexico; 266. Erik Ringoen, LB, Hofstra; 297. Tony Stewart, RB, Iowa; 324. Ike Harris, G, S. Carolina.

Tampa Bay Buccaneers

7. Charles McRae, T, Tennessee; 66. Lawrence Dawsey, WR, Florida St.; 80. Robert Wilson, RB, Texas A&M; 93. Tony Covington, DB, Virginia; 120. Terry Bagsby, RB, E. Texas St.; 136. Tim Ryan, G, Notre Dame; 147. Rhett Hall, DT, California; 174. Calvin Tiggle, LB, Georgia Tech; 207. Marty Carter, DB, Middle Tennessee St.; 233. Treamelle Taylor, WR, Nevada; 260. Pat O'Hara, QB, USC; 265. Hyland Hickson, RB, Michigan St.; 297. Mike Sunvold, DT, Minnesota; 314. Al Chamblee, LB, Louisiana Tech.

Washington Redskins

17. Bobby Wilson, DT, Michigan St.; 76. Ricky Ervins, RB, USC; 159. Dennis Ransom, TE, Texas A&M; 188. Keith Cash, WR, Texas; 215. Jimmy Spencer, DB, Florida; 243. Charles Bell, DB, Baylor; 270. Chris Shale, P, Bowling Green; 299. Dave Gulledge, DB, Jacksonville St.; 326. Keenan McCardell, WR, UNLV.

1990
Statistics

Leading Rushers	Att.	Yards	Avg.	TDs
AFC				
Thomas, Buff.	271	1297	4.8	11
Butts, S.D.	265	1225	4.6	8
Humphrey, Den.	288	1202	4.2	7
Word, K.C.	204	1015	5.0	4
Brooks, Cin.	195	1004	5.1	5
Fenner, Sea.	215	859	4.0	14
Smith, Mia.	226	831	3.7	8
Stephens, N.E.	212	808	3.8	2
Okoye, K.C.	245	805	3.3	7
Hoge, Pitt.	203	772	3.8	7
Williams, Sea.	187	714	3.8	3
Mack, Clev.	158	702	4.4	5
White, Hou.	168	702	4.2	8
Jackson, Raiders	125	698	5.6	5
Allen, Raiders	179	682	3.8	12
Dickerson, Ind.	166	677	4.1	4
Thomas, Jets	123	620	5.0	1
Bernstine, S.D.	124	589	4.8	4
Bentley, Ind.	137	556	4.1	4
Baxter, Jets	124	539	4.3	6

Leading Rushers	Att.	Yards	Avg.	TDs
NFC				
Sanders, Det.	255	1304	5.1	13
Byner, Wash.	297	1219	4.1	6
Anderson, Chi.	260	1078	4.1	10
Cunningham, Phil.	118	942	8.0	5
Smith, Dall.	241	937	3.9	11
Johnson, Phoe.	234	926	4.0	5
Gary, Rams	204	808	4.0	14
Anderson, Giants	225	784	3.5	11
Walker, Minn.	184	770	4.2	5
Rozier, Hou.-Atl.	163	717	4.4	3
Sherman, Phil.	164	685	4.2	1
Muster, Chi.	141	664	4.7	6
Anderson, T.B.	166	646	3.9	3
Heyward, N.O.	129	599	4.6	4
Mayes, N.O.	138	510	3.7	7
Cobb, T.B.	151	480	3.2	2
Riggs, Wash.	123	475	3.9	6

Leading Passers	Att.	Comp.	Yds. Gnd.	TD Pass	Int.	Rat- ing
AFC						
Kelly, Buff.	346	219	2829	24	9	101.2
Moon, Hou.	584	362	4689	33	13	96.8
DeBerg, K.C.	444	258	3444	23	4	96.3
Schroeder, Raiders	334	182	2849	19	9	90.8
Marino, Mia.	531	306	3563	21	11	82.6
Brister, Pitt.	387	223	2725	20	14	81.6
Elway, Den.	502	294	3526	15	14	78.5
O'Brien, Jets	411	226	2855	13	10	77.3
Esiason, Cin.	402	224	3031	24	22	77.0
George, Ind.	334	181	2152	16	13	73.8
Krieg, Sea.	448	265	3194	15	20	73.6
Tolliver, S.D.	410	216	2574	16	16	68.9
Kosar, Clev.	423	230	2562	10	15	65.7
Wilson, N.E.	265	139	1625	6	11	61.6

Leading Passers	Att.	Comp.	Yds. Gnd.	TD Pass	Int.	Rat- ing
NFC						
Simms, Giants	311	184	2284	15	4	92.7
Cunningham, Phil.	465	271	3466	30	13	91.6
Montana, S.F.	520	321	3944	26	16	89.0
Harbaugh, Chi.	312	180	2178	10	6	81.9
Peete, Det.	271	142	1974	13	8	79.8
Everett, Rams	554	307	3989	23	17	79.3
Miller, Atl.	388	222	2735	17	14	78.7
Rypien, Wash.	304	166	2070	16	11	78.4
Testaverde, T.B.	365	203	2818	17	18	75.6
Majkowski, G.B.	264	150	1925	10	12	73.5
Rosenbach, Phoe.	437	237	3098	16	17	72.8
Gannon, Minn.	349	182	2278	16	16	68.9
Walsh, Dall.-N.O.	336	179	2010	12	13	67.2
Aikman, Dall.	399	226	2579	11	18	66.6

Leading Receivers	No.	Yards	Avg.	TDs
AFC				
Jeffires, Hou.	74	1048	14.2	8
Hill, Hou.	74	1019	13.8	5
Williams, Sea.	73	699	9.6	0
Givins, Hou.	72	979	13.6	9
Reed, Buff.	71	945	13.3	8
Bentley, Ind.	71	664	9.4	2
Duncan, Hou.	66	785	11.9	1
Paige, K.C.	65	1021	15.7	5
Miller, S.D.	63	933	14.8	7
Brooks, Ind.	62	823	13.3	5
Slaughter, Clev.	59	847	14.4	4
Jackson, Den.	57	926	16.2	4
Toon, Jets	57	757	13.3	6
Metcalf, Clev.	57	452	7.9	1
Hester, Ind.	54	924	17.1	6
Fryar, N.E.	54	856	15.9	4
Johnson, Den.	54	747	13.8	3

Leading Receivers	No.	Yards	Avg.	TDs
NFC				
Rice, S.F.	100	1502	15.0	13
Rison, Atl.	82	1208	14.7	10
Byars, Phil.	81	819	10.1	3
Ellard, Rams	76	1294	17.0	4
Clark, Wash.	75	1112	14.8	8
Carter, Minn.	70	1008	14.4	8
Monk, Wash.	68	770	11.3	5
Sharpe, G.B.	67	1105	16.5	6
Martin, Dall.	64	732	11.4	0
Johnson, Det.	64	727	11.4	6
Martin, N.O.	63	912	14.5	5
Novacek, Dall.	59	657	11.1	4
Proehl, Phoe.	56	802	14.3	4
Jones, S.F.	56	747	13.3	5
Sanders, Wash.	56	727	13.0	3
Green, Phoe.	53	797	15.0	4
Clark, Det.	52	914	17.6	8

Leading Interceptors	No.	Yards	Long	TDs
AFC				
Johnson, Hou.	8	100	35	1
Byrd, S.D.	7	63	24	0
Ross, K.C.	5	97	40	0
McMillan, Jets	5	92	25	0
Oliver, Mia.	5	87	35	0
Williams, Mia.	5	82	42	1
Woodson, Pitt.	5	67	34	0
NFC				
Carrier, Chi.	10	39	14	0
Haddix, T.B.	7	231	65	3
Browner, Minn.	7	103	31	1
Waymer, S.F.	7	64	24	0
Mayhew, Wash.	7	20	15	0
Walls, Giants	6	80	40	1
Stinson, Chi.	6	66	30	0

Leading Scorers, Kicking	XP	XPA	FG	FGA	Pts.
AFC					
Lowery, K.C.	37	38	34	37	139
Norwood, Buff.	50	52	20	29	110
Treadwell, Den.	34	36	25	34	109
Johnson, Sea.	33	34	23	32	102
Leahy, Jets	32	32	23	26	101
Stoyanovich, Mia.	37	37	21	25	100
Anderson, Pitt.	32	32	20	25	92
Breech, Cin.	41	44	17	21	92
NFC					
Lohmiller, Wash.	41	41	30	40	131
Butler, Chi.	36	37	26	37	114
Cofer, S.F.	39	39	24	36	111
Ruzek, Phil.	45	48	21	29	108
Davis, Atl.	40	40	22	33	106
Jacke, G.B.	28	29	23	30	97
Christie, T.B.	27	27	23	27	96
Andersen, N.O.	29	29	21	27	92

Leading Scorers, Touchdowns	TDs	Rush	Rec.	Ret.	Pts.
AFC					
Fenner, Sea.	15	14	1	0	90
Allen, Raiders	13	12	1	0	78
Thomas, Buff.	13	11	2	0	78
White, Hou.	12	8	4	0	72
Hoge, Pitt.	10	7	3	0	60
Brooks, Cin.	9	5	4	0	54
Brown, Cin.	9	0	9	0	54
Givins, Hou.	9	0	9	0	54
Smith, Mia.	9	8	1	0	54
Butts, S.D.	8	8	0	0	48
Jeffires, Hou.	8	0	8	0	48
Reed, Buff.	8	0	8	0	48
Green, Pitt.	7	0	7	0	42
Humphrey, Den.	7	7	0	0	42
Mack, Clev.	7	5	2	0	42

Leading Scorers, Touchdowns	TDs	Rush	Rec.	Ret.	Pts.
NFC					
Sanders, Det.	16	13	3	0	96
Gary, Rams	15	14	1	0	90
Anderson, Chi.	13	10	3	0	78
Rice, S.F.	13	0	13	0	78
Anderson, Giants	11	11	0	0	66
Smith, Dall.	11	11	0	0	66
Rison, Atl.	10	0	10	0	60
Walker, Minn.	9	5	4	0	54
Williams, Phil.	9	0	9	0	54
Barnett, Phil.	8	0	8	0	48
Carter, Minn.	8	0	8	0	48
Clark, Wash.	8	0	8	0	48
Clark, Det.	8	0	8	0	48
Byner, Wash.	7	6	1	0	42
Jones, Minn.	7	0	7	0	42
Mayes, N.O.	7	7	0	0	42
Rathman, S.F.	7	7	0	0	42
Taylor, S.F.	7	0	7	0	42

Leading Punters	No.	Yards	Long	Avg.
AFC				
Horan, Den.	58	2575	67	44.4
Stark, Ind.	71	3084	61	43.4
Johnson, Cin.	64	2705	70	42.3
Roby, Mia.	72	3022	62	42.0
Hansen, N.E.	90	3752	69	41.7
Donnelly, Sea.	67	2722	54	40.6
Prokop, Jets	59	2363	58	40.1
Kidd, S.D.	61	2442	59	40.0
Tuten, Buff.	53	2107	55	39.8
Wagner, Clev.	74	2879	65	38.9
Barker, K.C.	64	2479	56	38.7
Gossett, Raiders	60	2315	57	38.6
Stryzinski, Pitt.	65	2454	51	37.8

Leading Punters	No.	Yards	Long	Avg.
NFC				
Landeta, Giants	75	3306	67	44.1
Saxon, Dall.	79	3413	62	43.2
Camarillo, Phoe.	67	2865	63	42.8
Barnhardt, N.O.	70	2990	65	42.7
Newsome, Minn.	78	3299	61	42.3
Feagles, Phil.	72	3026	60	42.0
Fulhage, Atl.	70	2913	59	41.6
Arnold, Det.	63	2560	59	40.6
Buford, Chi.	76	3073	59	40.4
Royals, T.B.	72	2902	62	40.3
Mojsiejenko, Wash.	43	1687	53	39.2
English, Rams	68	2663	58	39.2
Bracken, G.B.	64	2431	59	38.0
Helton, S.F.	69	2537	56	36.8

Leading Punt Returners	No.	Yards	Avg.	TDs
AFC				
Verdin, Ind.	31	396	12.8	0
Woodson, Pitt.	38	398	10.5	1
Warren, Sea.	28	269	9.6	0
Brown, Raiders	34	295	8.7	0
Price, Cin.	29	251	8.7	1
Clark, Den.	21	159	7.6	0
Worthen, K.C.	25	180	7.2	0
McNeil, Hou.	30	172	5.7	0
NFC				
Bailey, Chi.	36	399	11.1	1
Meggett, Giants	43	467	10.9	1
Gray, Det.	34	361	10.6	0
Query, G.B.	32	308	9.6	0
Sanders, Atl.	29	250	8.6	1
Sikahema, Phoe.	36	306	8.5	0
Buck, N.O.	37	305	8.2	0
Taylor, S.F.	26	212	8.2	0
Drewrey, T.B.	23	184	8.0	0

Leading Kickoff Returners	No.	Yards	Avg.	TDs
AFC				
Clark, Den.	20	505	25.3	0
Elder, S.D.	24	571	23.8	0
Woodson, Pitt.	35	764	21.8	0
Warren, Sea.	23	478	20.8	0
Martin, N.E.	25	515	20.6	0
Holland, Raiders	32	655	20.5	0
McNeil, Hou.	27	551	20.4	0
Metcalf, Clev.	52	1052	20.2	2
Jennings, Cin.	29	584	20.1	0
Smith, Buff.	32	643	20.1	0
Brown, Raiders	30	575	19.2	0
Logan, Mia.	20	367	18.4	0
Mathis, Jets	43	787	18.3	0
NFC				
Meggett, Giants	21	492	23.4	0
Gray, Det.	41	939	22.9	0
Wilson, G.B.	35	798	22.8	0
Green, Rams	25	560	22.4	1
Walker, Minn.	44	966	22.0	0
Sanders, Atl.	39	851	21.8	0
Dixon, Dall.	36	736	20.4	0
Fenerty, N.O.	28	572	20.4	0
Sikahema, Phoe.	27	544	20.1	0
Delpino, Rams	20	389	19.5	0
Howard, Wash.	22	427	19.4	0
Carter, S.F.	41	783	19.1	0
Hampton, Giants	20	340	17.0	0
Bailey, Chi.	23	363	15.8	0

1991
NFL Schedule

Sunday, September 1
Miami at Buffalo
Cincinnati at Denver
Dallas at Cleveland
L.A. Raiders at Houston
New Eng. at Indianapolis
Atlanta at Kansas City
Tampa Bay at N.Y. Jets
San Diego at Pittsburgh
Seattle at New Orleans
Minnesota at Chicago
Detroit at Washington
Phil. at Green Bay
Phoenix at L.A. Rams

Monday, September 2
San Fran. at N.Y. Giants

Sunday, September 8
Pittsburgh at Buffalo
Houston at Cincinnati
Cleveland at New England
Denver at L.A. Raiders
Indianapolis at Miami
New Orl. at Kansas City
N.Y. Jets at Seattle
San Diego at San Fran.
Minnesota at Atlanta
Chicago at Tampa Bay
Green Bay at Detroit
L.A. Rams at N.Y. Giants
Phoenix at Philadelphia

Monday, September 9
Washington at Dallas

Sunday, September 15
Buffalo at N.Y. Jets
Cincinnati at Cleveland
Seattle at Denver
Indianap. at L.A. Raiders
Miami at Detroit
New England at Pittsburgh
Atlanta at San Diego
N.Y. Giants at Chicago
Philadelphia at Dallas
Tampa Bay at Green Bay
L.A. Rams at New Orleans
San Fran. at Minnesota
Phoenix at Washington

Monday, September 16
Kansas City at Houston

Sunday, September 22
Buffalo at Tampa Bay
Washington at Cincinnati
Cleveland at N.Y. Giants
San Diego at Denver
Houston at New England
Detroit at Indianapolis
Seattle at Kansas City
L.A. Raiders at Atlanta
Green Bay at Miami
Pittsburgh at Phil.
Dallas at Phoenix
L.A. Rams at San Fran.
Minnesota at New Orleans

Monday, September 23
N.Y. Jets at Chicago

Sunday, September 29
Chicago at Buffalo
Washington at Cincinnati
Indianapolis at Seattle
Kansas City at San Diego
San Fran. at L.A. Raiders
Miami at N.Y. Jets
New England at Phoenix
New Orleans at Atlanta
N.Y. Giants at Dallas
Tampa Bay at Detroit
Green Bay at L.A. Rams
Denver at Minnesota

Monday, September 30
Phil. at Washington

Sunday, October 6
Seattle at Cincinnati
N.Y. Jets at Cleveland
Denver at Houston
Pittsburgh at Indianap.
San Diego at L.A. Raiders
Miami at New England
Washington at Chicago
Dallas vs. Green Bay
   at Milwaukee
Minnesota at Detroit
Phoenix at N.Y. Giants
Phil. at Tampa Bay

Monday, October 7
Buffalo at Kansas City

Sunday, October 13
Indianapolis at Buffalo
Cincinnati at Dallas
Cleveland at Washington
Houston at N.Y. Jets
Miami at Kansas City
L.A. Raiders at Seattle

San Diego at L.A. Rams
San Francisco at Atlanta
Phoenix at Minnesota
New Orl. at Philadelphia

Monday, October 14
N.Y. Giants at Pittsburgh

Thursday, October 17
Chicago at Green Bay

Sunday, October 20
Houston at Miami
N.Y. Jets at Indianapolis
Seattle at Pittsburgh
Minnesota at New England
Tampa Bay at New Orleans
Atlanta at Phoenix
Cleveland at San Diego
Detroit at San Francisco
Kansas City at Denver
L.A. Rams at L.A. Raiders

Monday, October 21
Cincinnati at Buffalo

Sunday, October 27
Chicago at New Orleans
Cincinnati at Houston
Denver at New England
Green Bay at Tampa Bay
L.A. Rams at Atlanta
Pittsburgh at Cleveland
San Fran. at Philadelphia
Dallas at Detroit
Minnesota at Phoenix
San Diego at Seattle
Washington at N.Y. Giants

Monday, October 28
L.A. Raiders at Kan. City

Sunday, November 3
Cleveland at Cincinnati
Detroit at Chicago
Green Bay at N.Y. Jets
Houston at Washington
New England at Buffalo
Phoenix at Dallas
Tampa Bay at Minnesota
New Orleans at L.A. Rams
Miami at Indianapolis
Atlanta at San Francisco
Pittsburgh at Denver

Monday, November 4
N.Y. Giants at Phil.

Sunday, November 10
Atlanta at Washington
Buffalo vs. Green Bay
  at Milwaukee
Dallas at Houston
Detroit at Tampa Bay
Indianap. at N.Y. Jets
Philadelphia at Cleveland
Pittsburgh at Cincinnati
San Fran. at New Orleans
Kansas City at L.A. Rams
L.A. Raiders at Denver
N.Y. Giants at Phoenix
Seattle at San Diego
New England at Miami

Monday, November 11
Chicago at Minnesota

Sunday, November 17
Chicago at Indianapolis
Cincinnati at Philadelphia
Denver at Kansas City
Minnesota at Green Bay
N.Y. Jets at New England
Tampa Bay at Atlanta

Washington at Pittsburgh
Phoenix at San Francisco
L.A. Rams at Detroit
Dallas at N.Y. Giants
New Orleans at San Diego
Seattle at L.A. Raiders
Cleveland at Houston

Monday, November 18
Buffalo at Miami

Sunday, November 24
Buffalo at New England
Dallas at Washington
Detroit at Minnesota
Houston at Pittsburgh
Indianapolis vs. Green
  Bay at Milwaukee
Kansas City at Cleveland
L.A. Raiders at Cin.
Miami at Chicago
N.Y. Giants at Tampa Bay
Philadelphia at Phoenix
Denver at Seattle
San Diego at N.Y. Jets
Atlanta at New Orleans

Monday, November 25
San Fran. at L.A. Rams

Thursday, November 29
Chicago at Detroit
Pittsburgh at Dallas

Sunday, December 1
Cleveland at Indianapolis
Green Bay at Atlanta
N.Y. Jets at Buffalo
Tampa Bay at Miami
Kansas City at Seattle
New England at Denver
New Orleans at San Fran.

N.Y. Giants at Cincinnati
Washington at L.A. Rams
L.A. Raiders at San Diego

Monday, December 2
Philadelphia at Houston

Sunday, December 8
Denver at Cleveland
Green Bay at Chicago
Indianap. at New England
New Orleans at Dallas
Phil. at N.Y. Giants
Pittsburgh at Houston
San Diego at Kansas City
Atlanta at L.A. Rams
Buffalo at L.A. Raiders
N.Y. Jets at Detroit
San Francisco at Seattle
Washington at Phoenix
Minnesota at Tampa Bay

Monday, December 9
Cincinnati at Miami

Saturday, December 14
Tampa Bay at Chicago
Kansas City at San Fran.

Sunday, December 15
Cincinnati at Pittsburgh
Dallas at Philadelphia

Seattle at Atlanta
Detroit at Green Bay
Houston at Cleveland
L.A. Rams at Minnesota
New England at N.Y. Jets
N.Y. Giants at Washington
Miami at San Diego
Phoenix at Denver
Buffalo at Indianapolis

Monday, December 16
L.A. Raiders at New Orl.

Saturday, December 21
Houston at N.Y. Giants
Green Bay at Minnesota

Sunday, December 22
Atlanta at Dallas
Cleveland at Pittsburgh
Detroit at Buffalo
Indianapolis at Tampa Bay
New Eng. at Cincinnati
N.Y. Jets at Miami
Kan. City at L.A. Raiders
New Orleans at Phoenix
Denver at San Diego
Wash. at Philadelphia
L.A. Rams at Seattle

Monday, December 23
Chicago at San Francisco

BRUCE WEBER PICKS
HOW THEY'LL FINISH IN 1991

AFC East
1. Buffalo
2. Miami
3. N.Y. Jets
4. Indianapolis
5. New England

AFC Central
1. Houston
2. Pittsburgh
3. Cincinnati
4. Cleveland

AFC West
1. L.A. Raiders
2. Kansas City
3. Denver
4. Seattle
5. San Diego

NFC East
1. Washington
2. N.Y. Giants
3. Philadelphia
4. Dallas
5. Phoenix

NFC Central
1. Chicago
2. Minnesota
3. Green Bay
4. Detroit
5. Tampa Bay

NFC West
1. San Francisco
2. L.A. Rams
3. New Orleans
4. Atlanta

Wild Cards: Miami, Pittsburgh, Kansas City; N.Y. Giants, Minnesota, Philadelphia

AFC Champions: Buffalo
NFC Champions: San Francisco
Super Bowl Champions: Buffalo

YOU PICK
HOW THEY'LL FINISH IN 1991

AFC East
1. Bills
2. Dophits
3. Jets
4. Cots
5. Pairoits

NFC East
1. Dallas
2. Washington
3. Phili
4. New York
5. Cards

AFC Central
1. HOuston
2. Cleveland
3. Pittsburg
4. Cinnci

NFC Central
1. Bears
2. Detroit
3. Mhn
4. T Bay
5. G Bay

AFC West
1. Denver
2. Raiders
3. kansas City
4. Seatle
5. Chargers

NFC West
1. Fakong
2. San Fran
3. Saints
4. Rams

Wild Cards: San Fran, Ride San, Jets, PHi, Bills

AFC Champions: Bills

NFC Champions: Bears Dallas

Super Bowl Champions: DA BEA Dallas